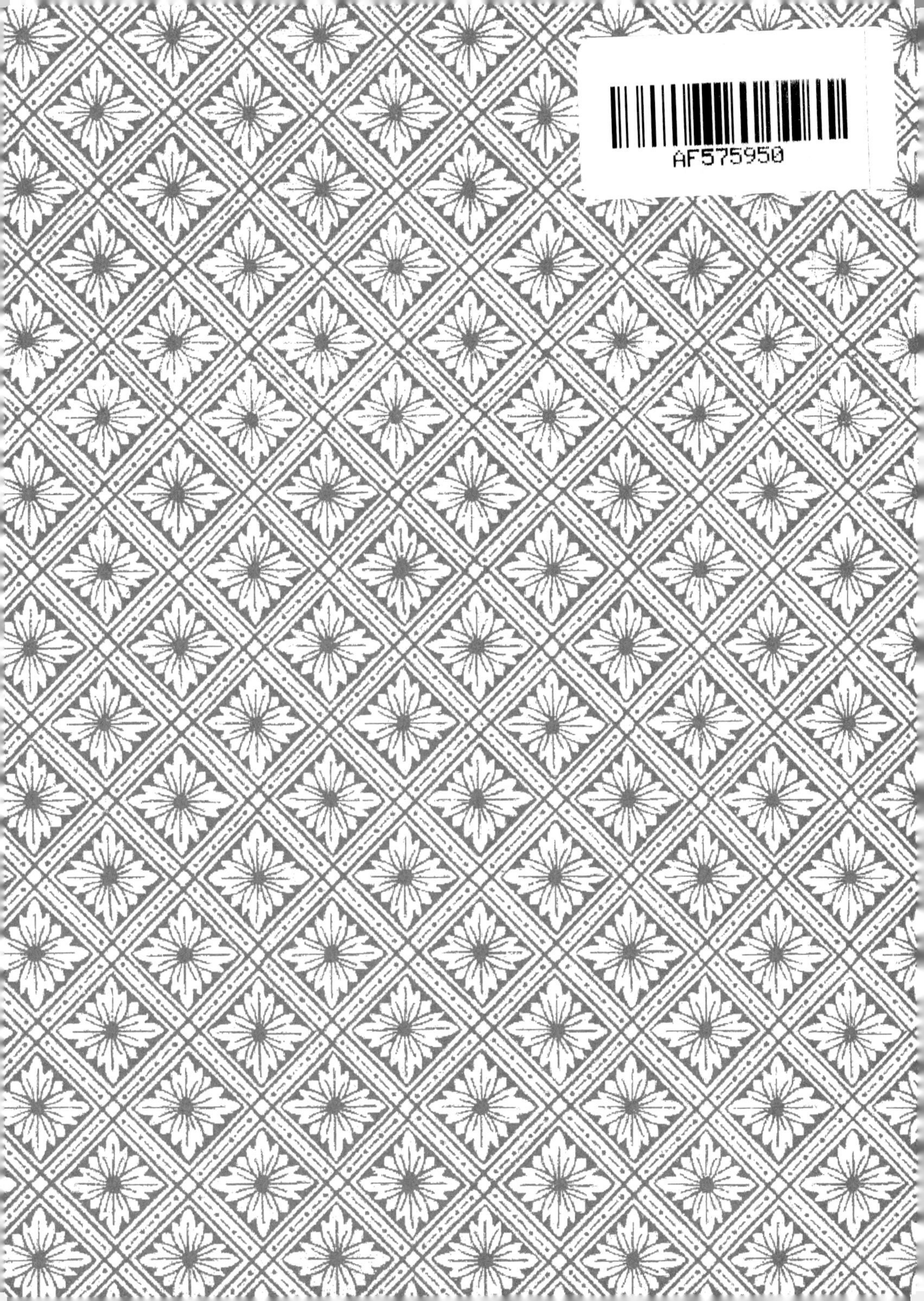

Fae Richards

THE FAE RICHARDS
PHOTO ARCHIVE

ZOE LEONARD PHOTOGRAPHER

CHERYL DUNYE FILMMAKER

ARTSPACE BOOKS

SAN FRANCISCO

AN ARTSPACE BOOKS ORIGINAL FIRST EDITION

BOOK AND COVER DESIGN BY KRISTIN JOHNSON

ISBN: 0-9631095-8-8

PRINTED IN HONG KONG

ARTSPACE BOOKS ARE AVAILABLE TO BOOKSTORES THROUGH OUR PRIMARY DISTRIBUTOR:
D.A.P./DISTRIBUTED ART PUBLISHERS, 155 AVENUE OF THE AMERICAS, 2ND FLOOR, NEW YORK NY 10013.
TELEPHONE: 212/627-1999 OR 800/338-BOOK. FOR PERSONAL ORDERS, PLEASE WRITE TO
ARTSPACE BOOKS 123 SOUTH PARK, SAN FRANCISCO, CA 94107.
TELEPHONE: 415-546-9100. FAX: 415-546-0236.

ARTSPACE BOOKS ARE PUBLISHED BY SAN FRANCISCO ARTSPACE, A NONPROFIT VIDEO PRODUCTION FACILITY AND PUBLISHING HOUSE.

ZOE LEONARD WOULD LIKE TO THANK

MARISA CARDINALE

CLAUDINE BENOIT

AND THE AMAZING CAST & CREW

CHERYL DUNYE WOULD LIKE TO THANK

ROBERT REID-PHARR

ALEX JUHASZ

AND HER MOTHER, EDITH DUNYE

The Fae Richards Photo Archive

~

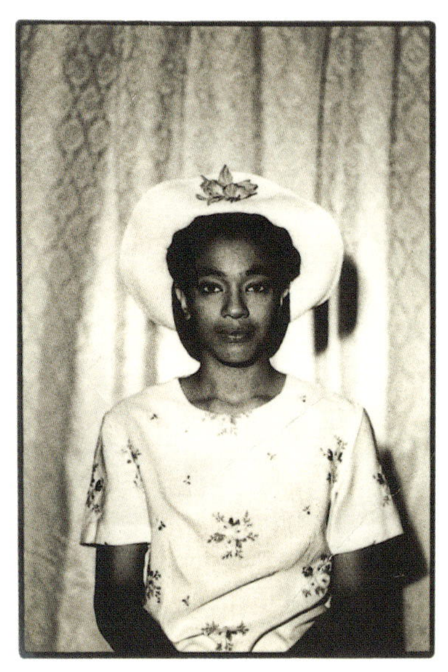

1

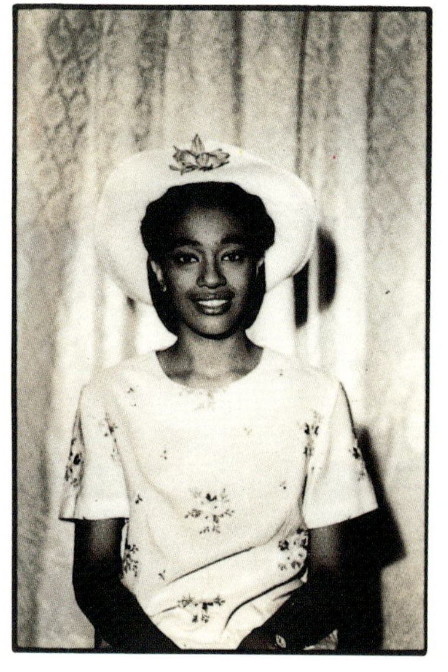

2

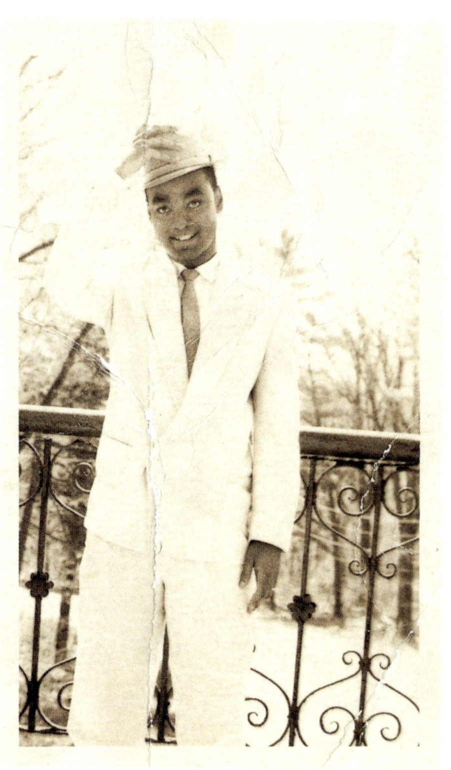

3

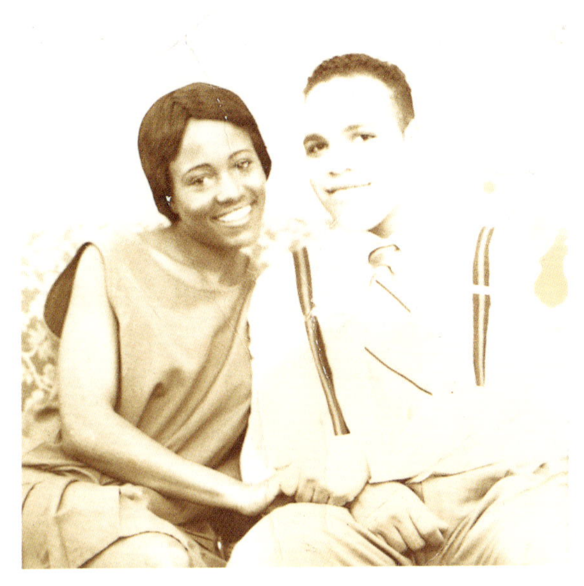

4

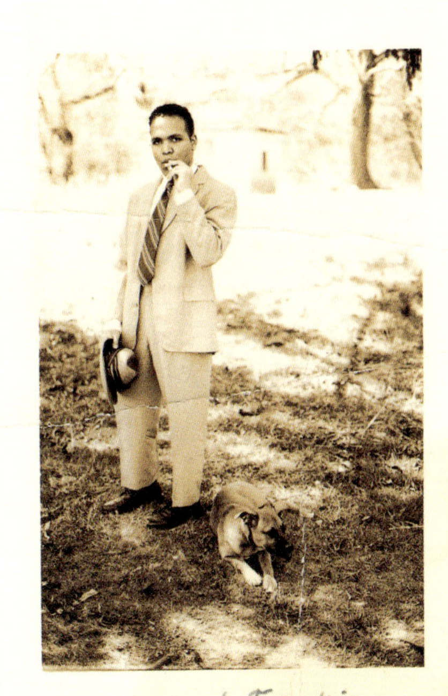

Oscar and Frankie

5

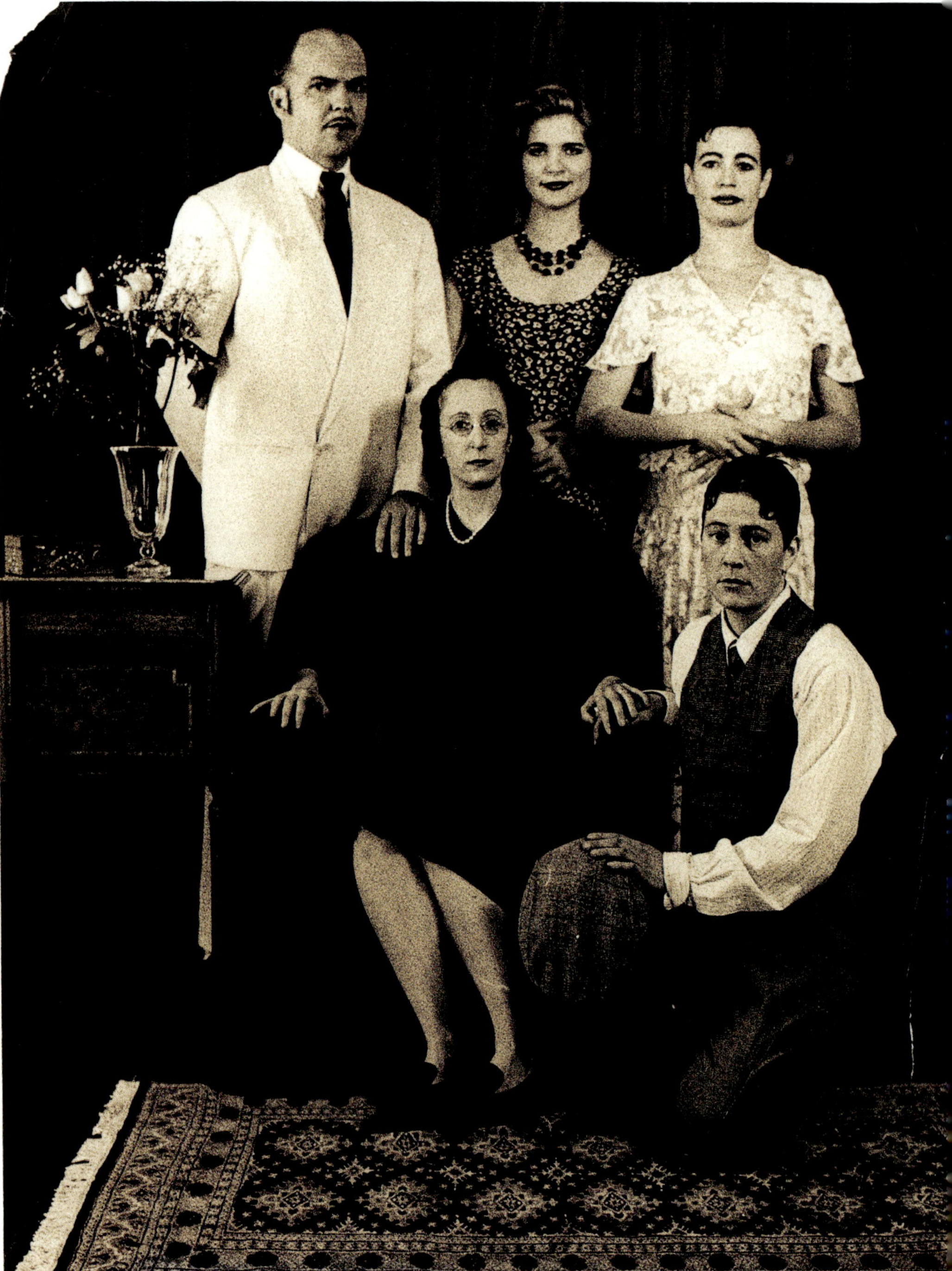

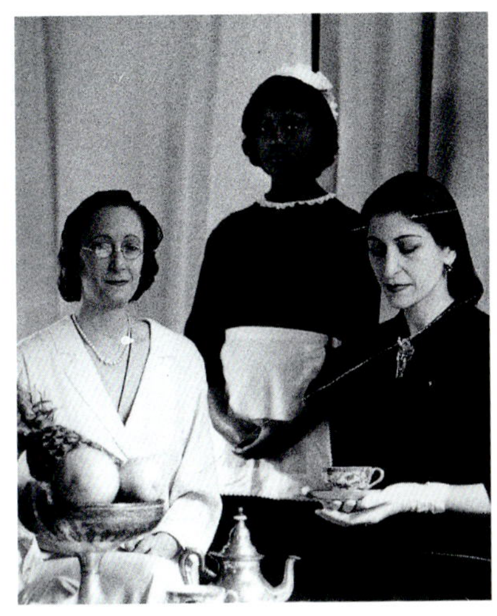

7

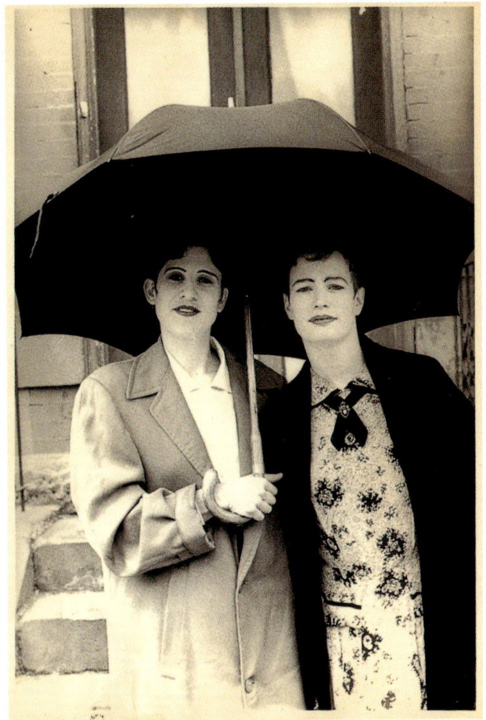

8

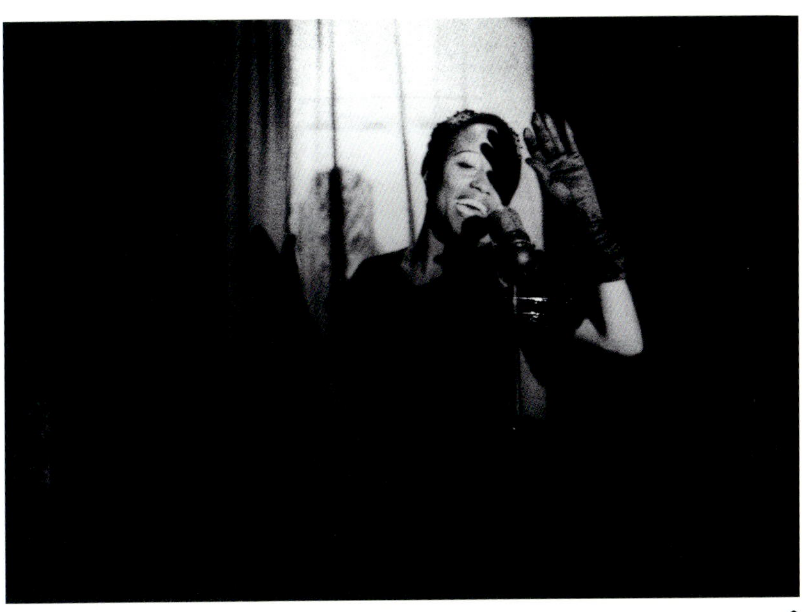

9

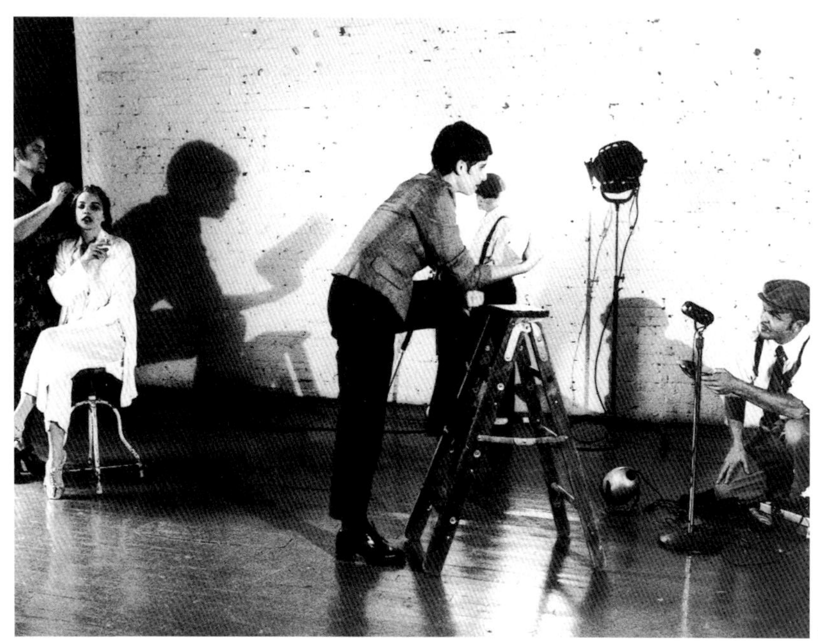

10

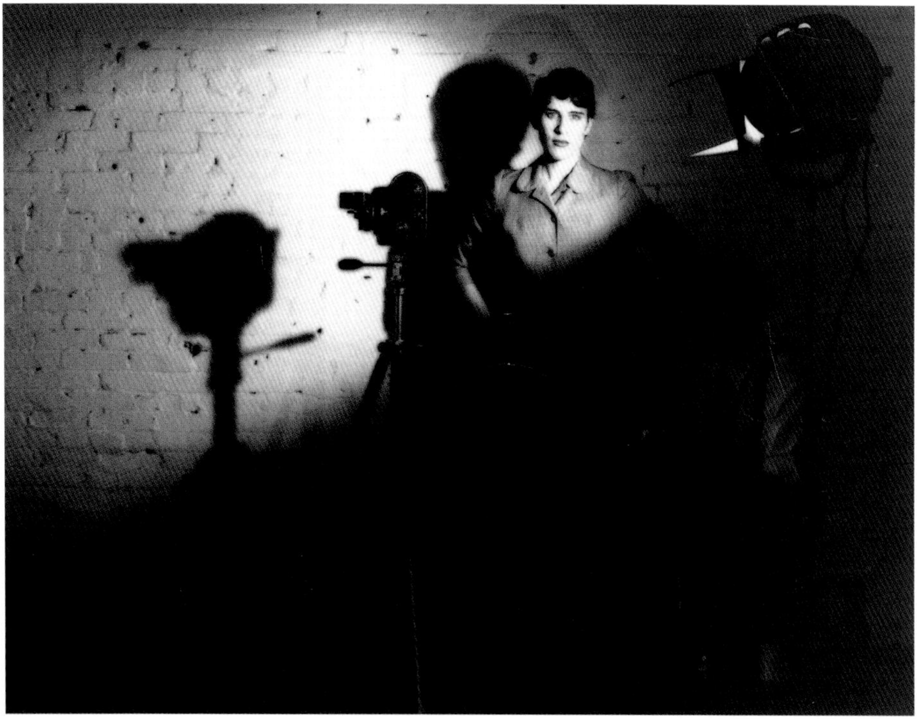

11

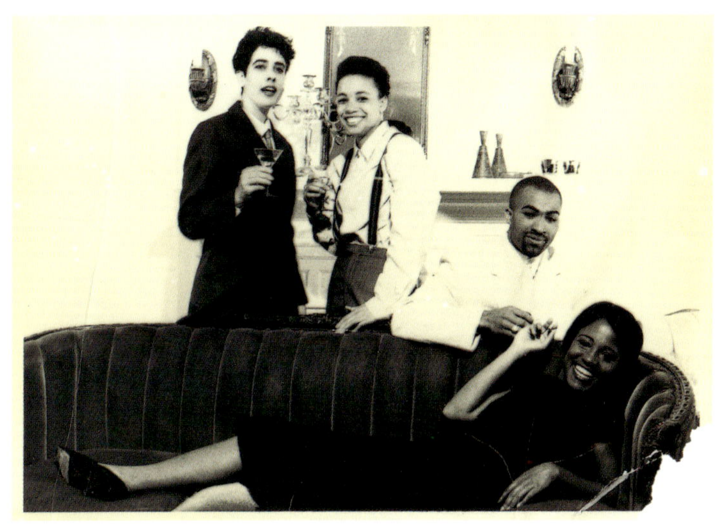

12

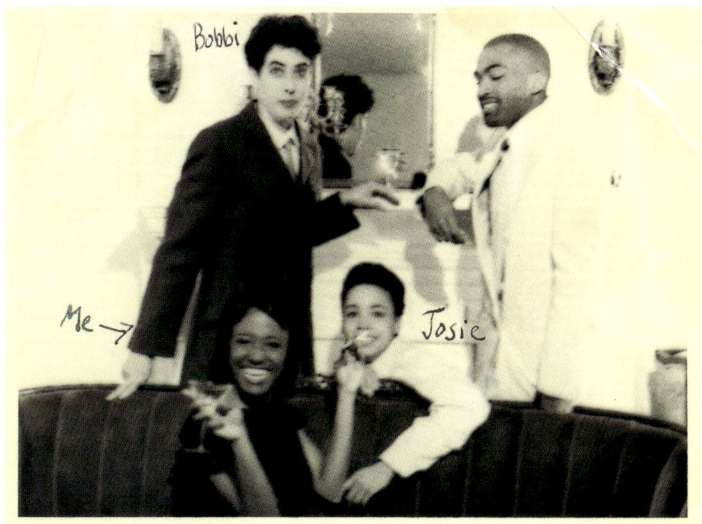

13

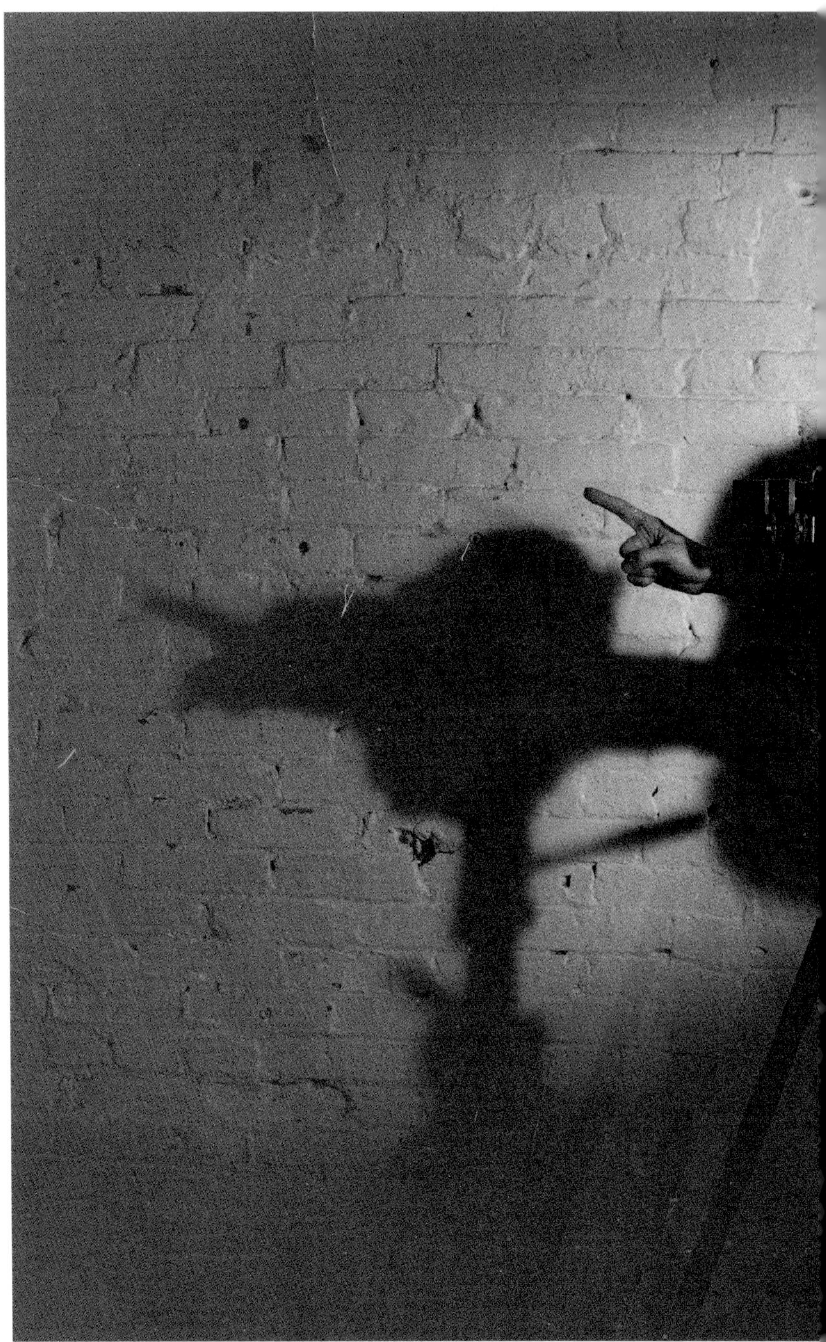

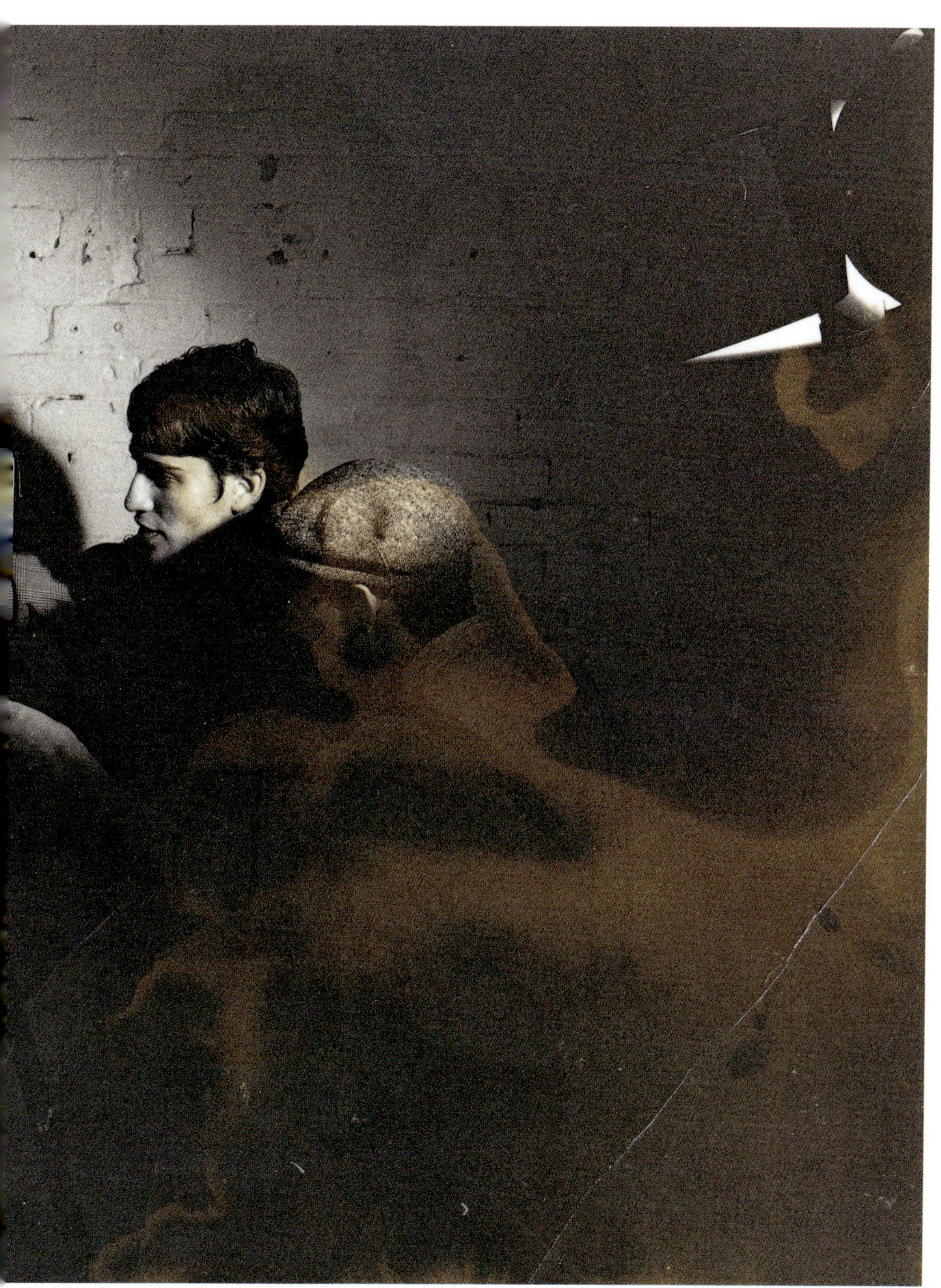

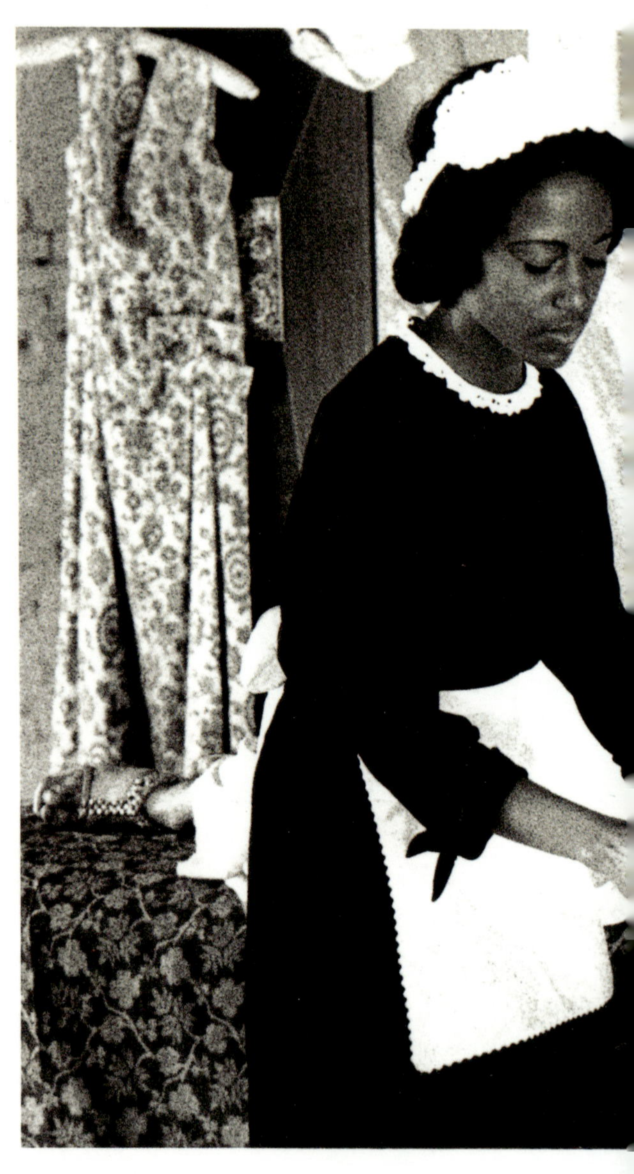

Sandra Vincent and Fae Richards i

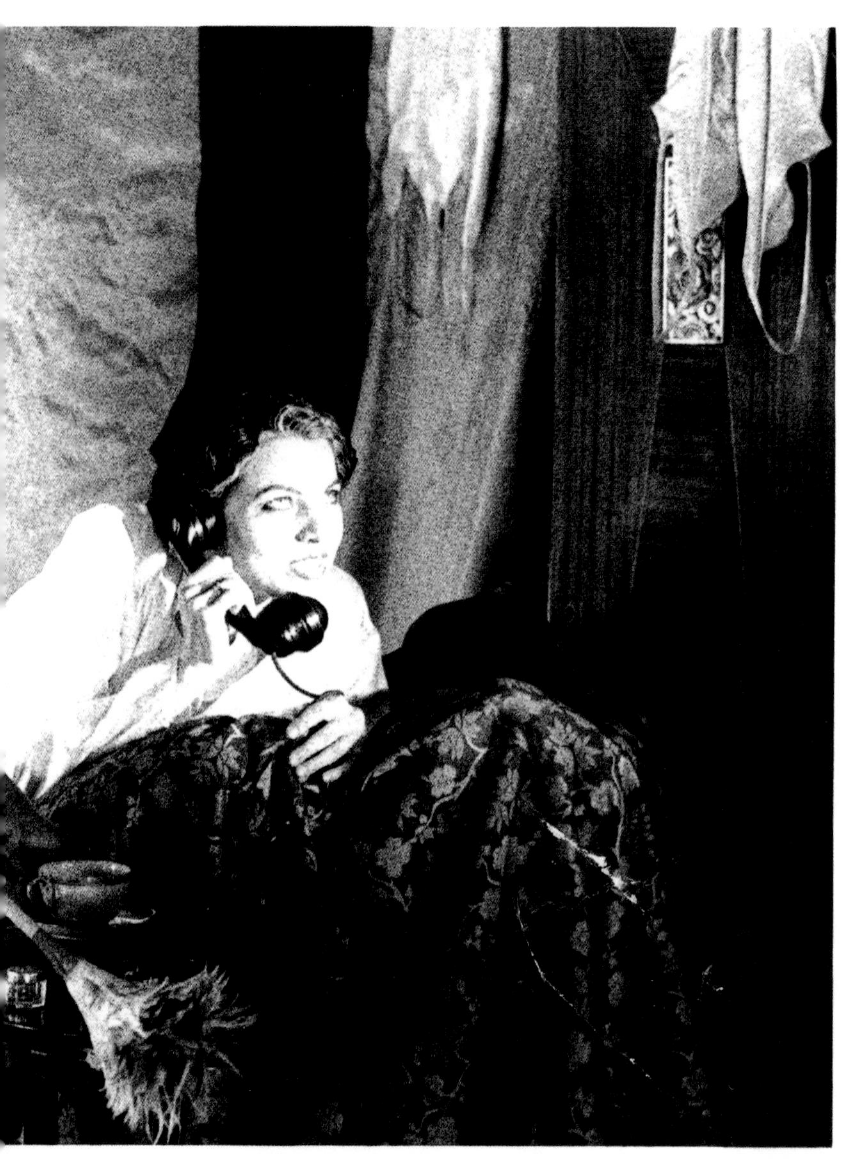

sey Girl", A Newark Studio Productio . 1931

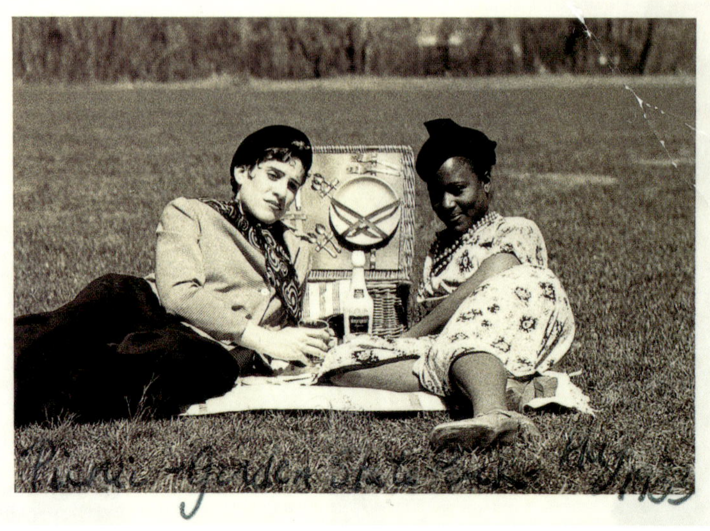

16

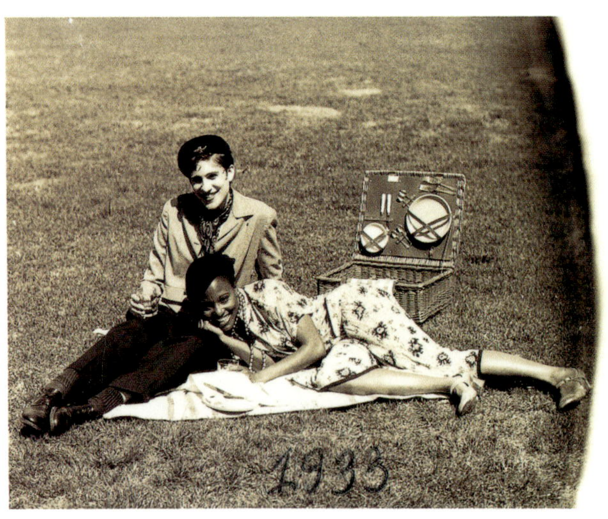

17

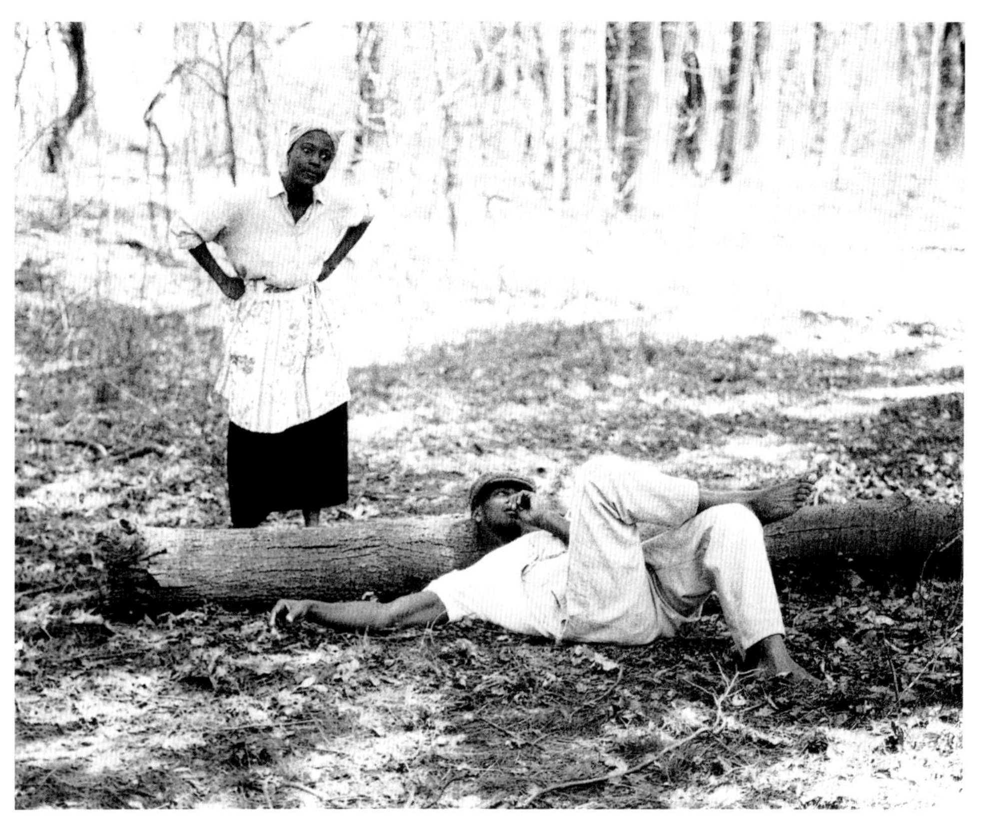

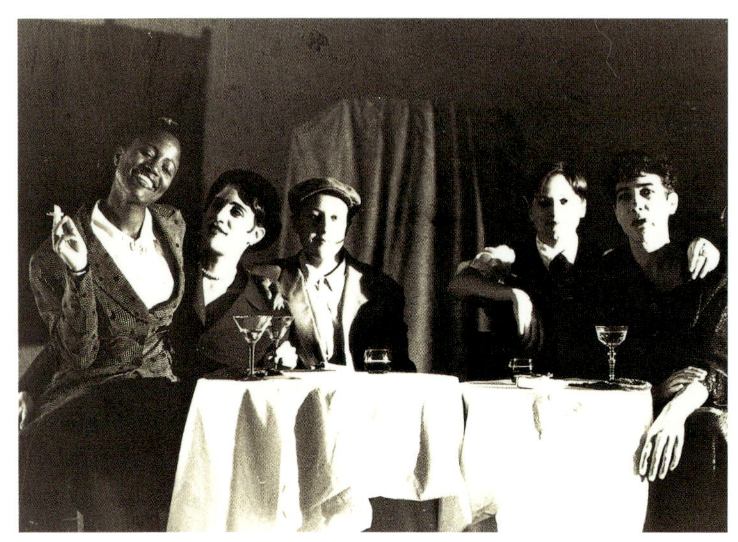

19

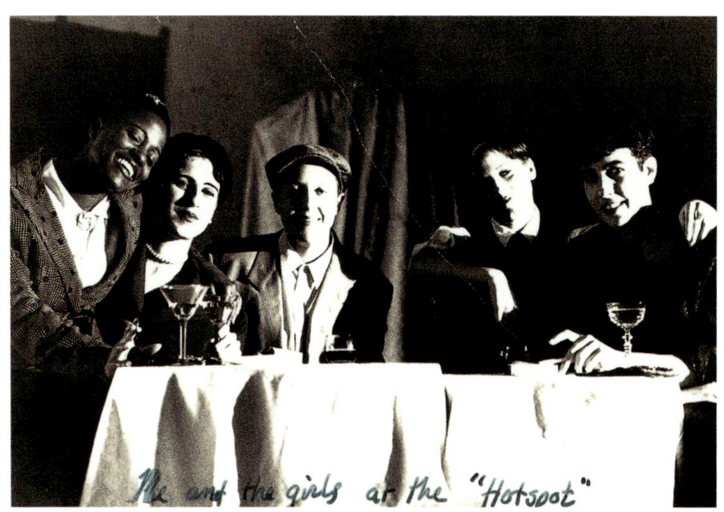

20

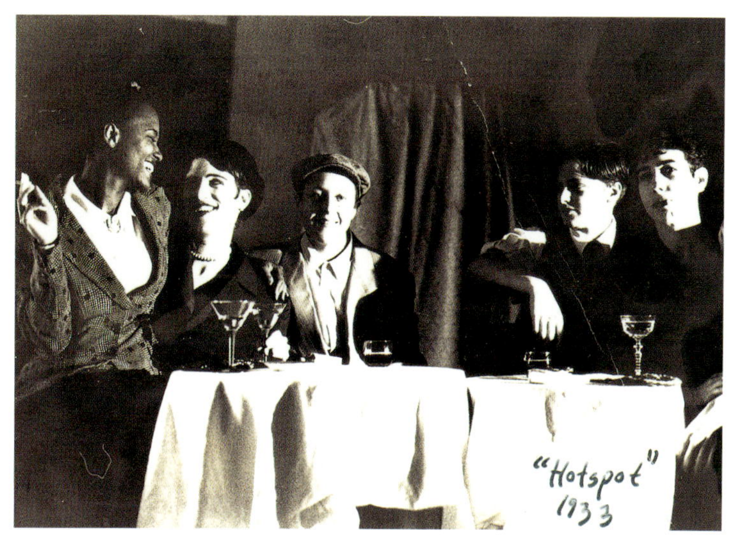

21

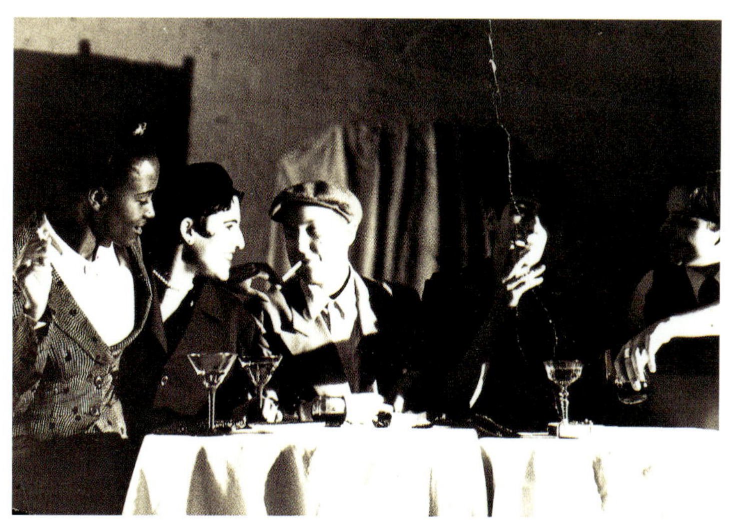

22

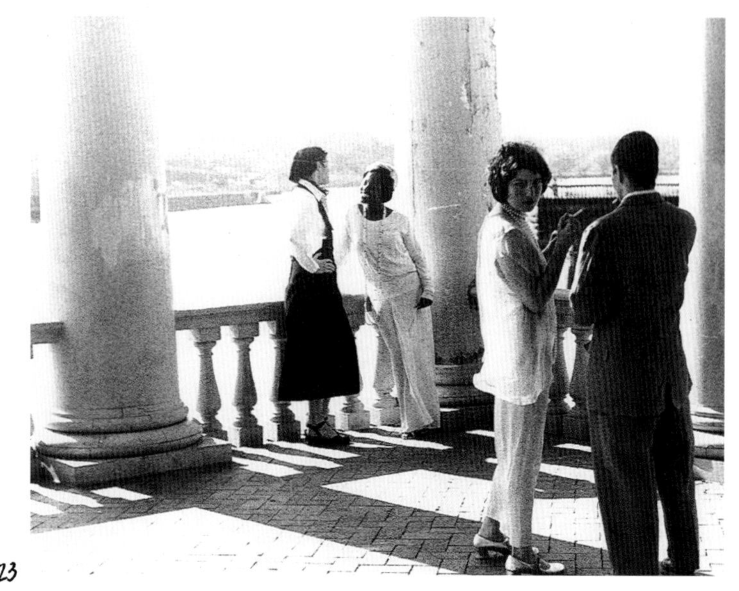

23

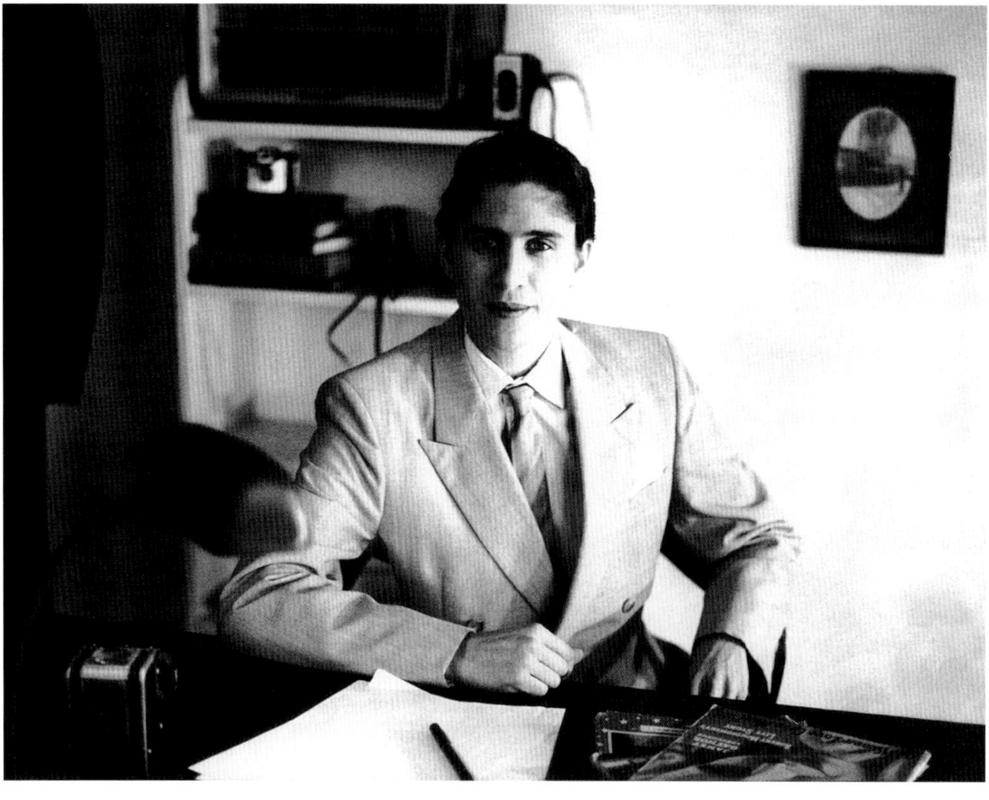

24

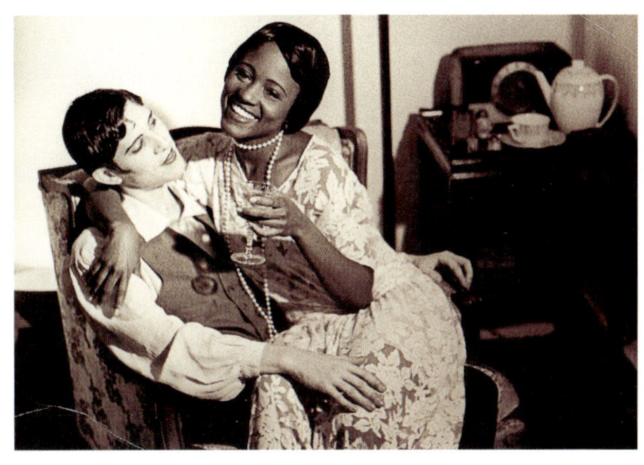

25

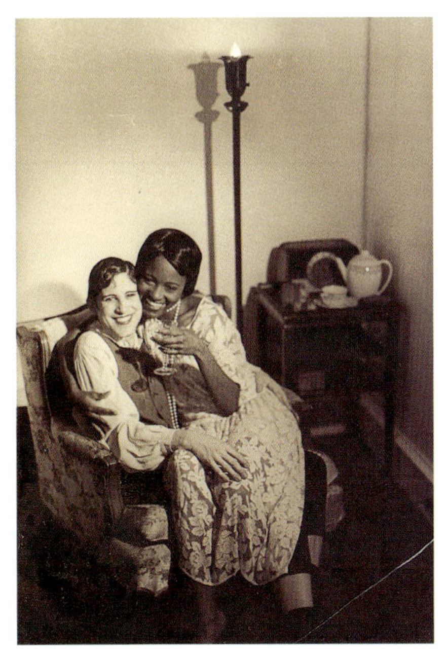

26

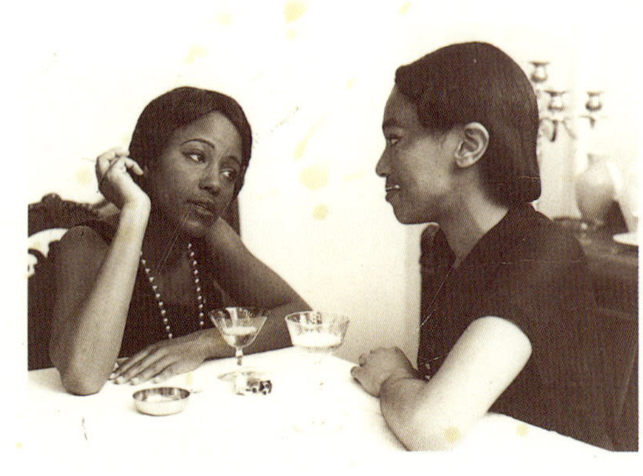

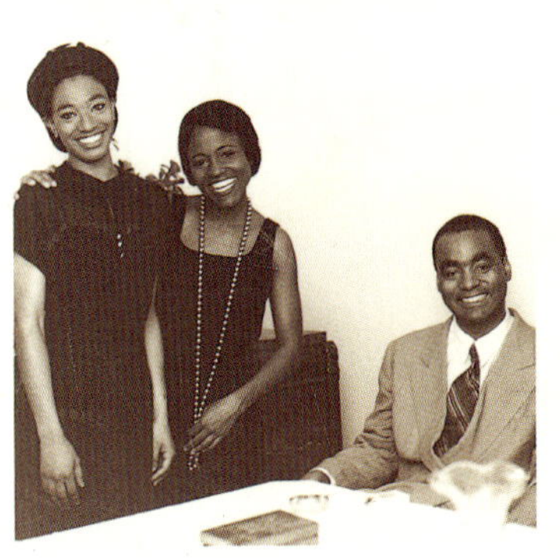

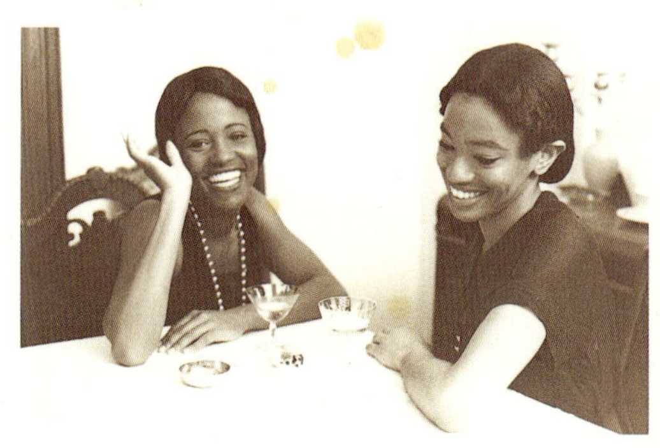

27 - 30

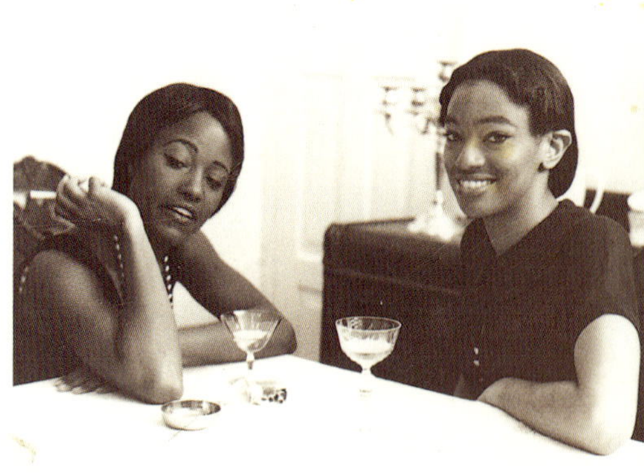

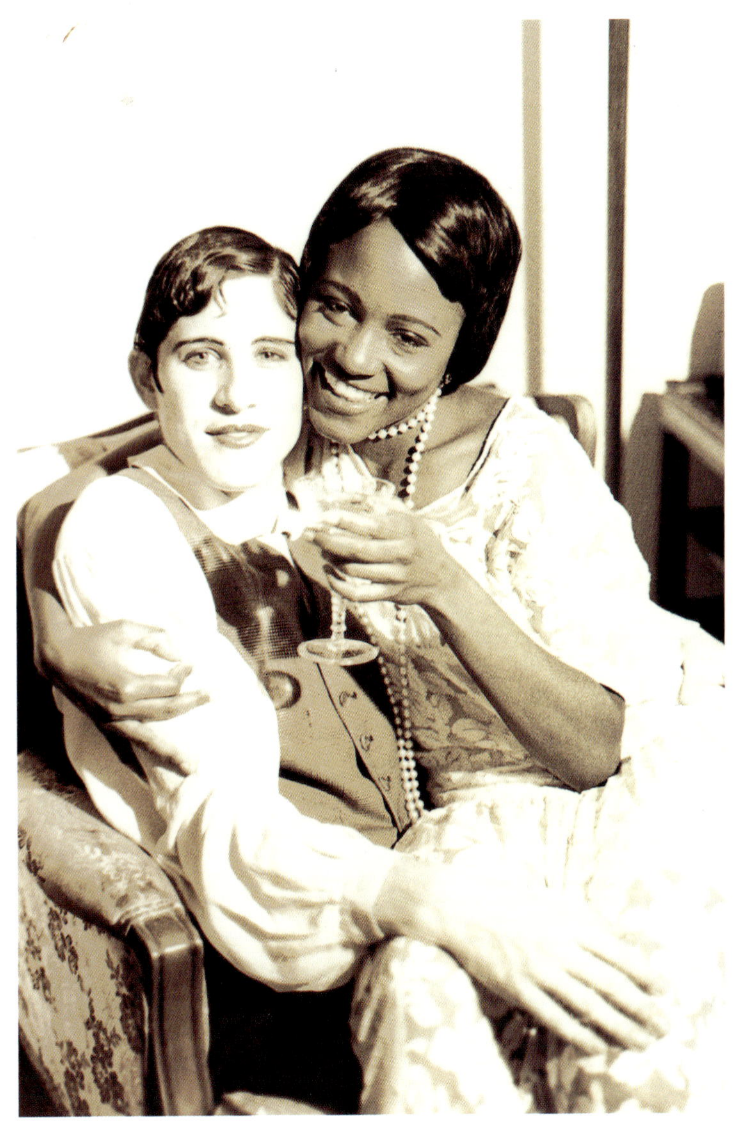

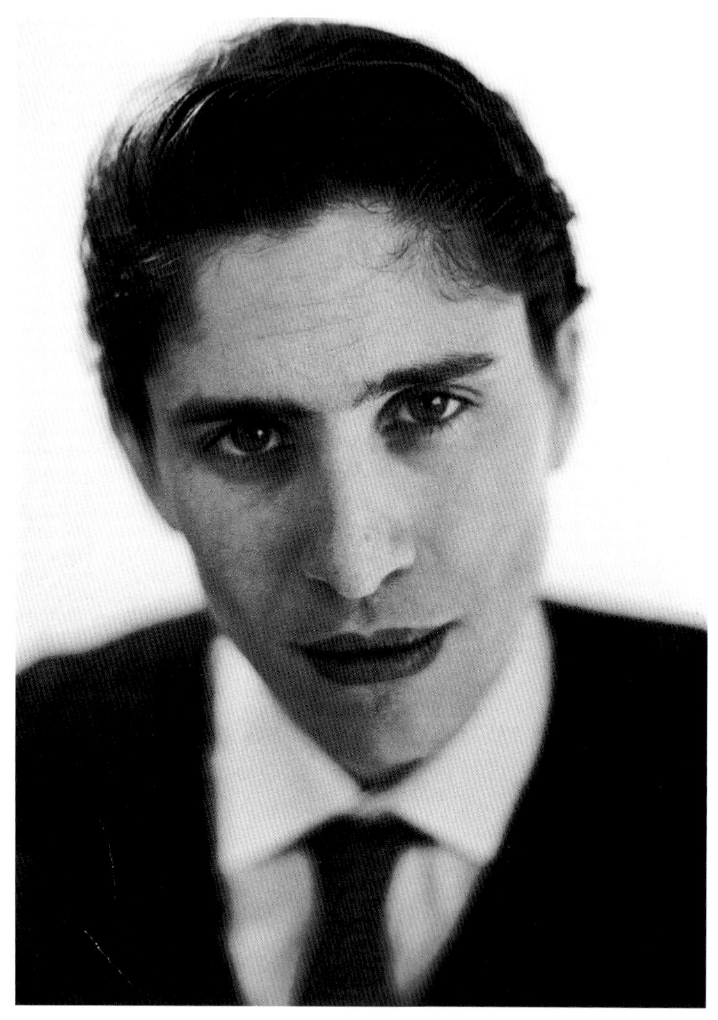

32

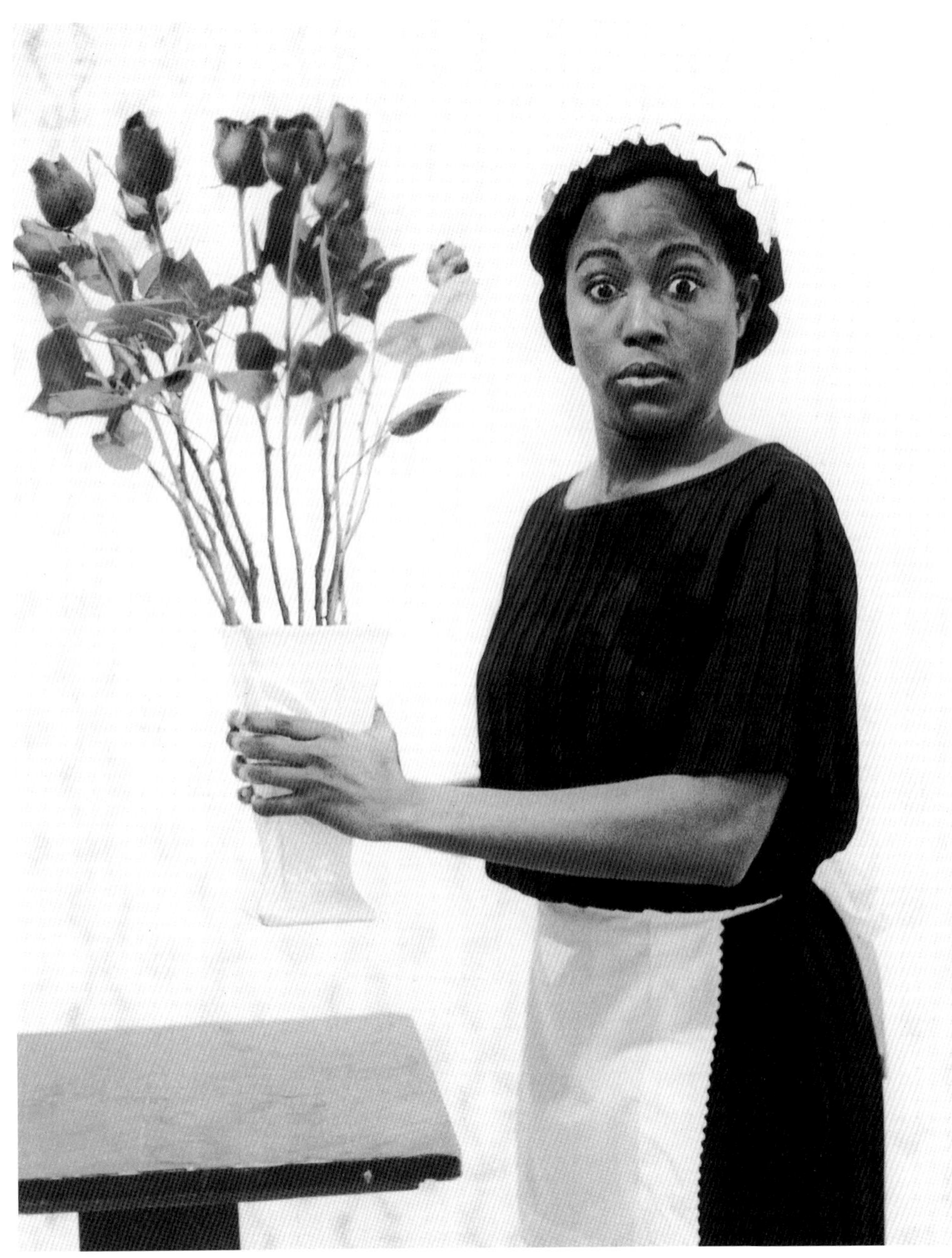

34

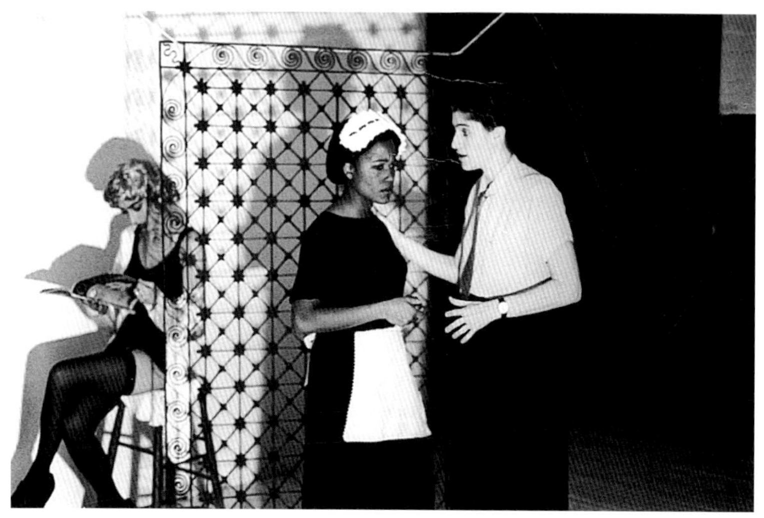

35

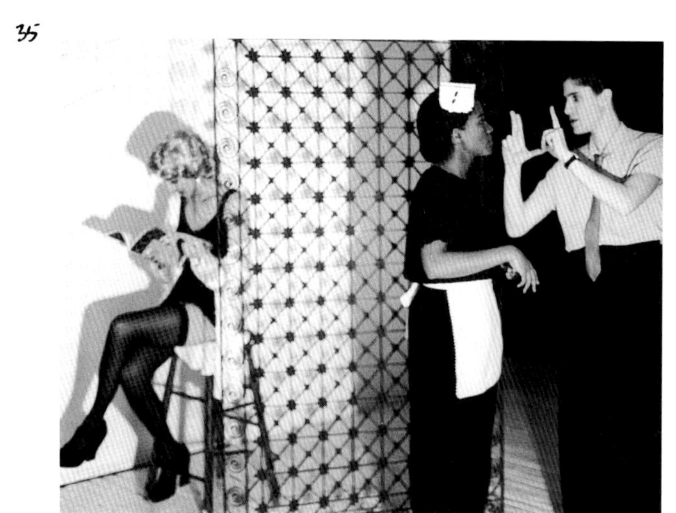

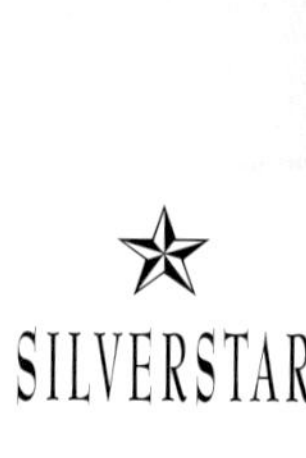

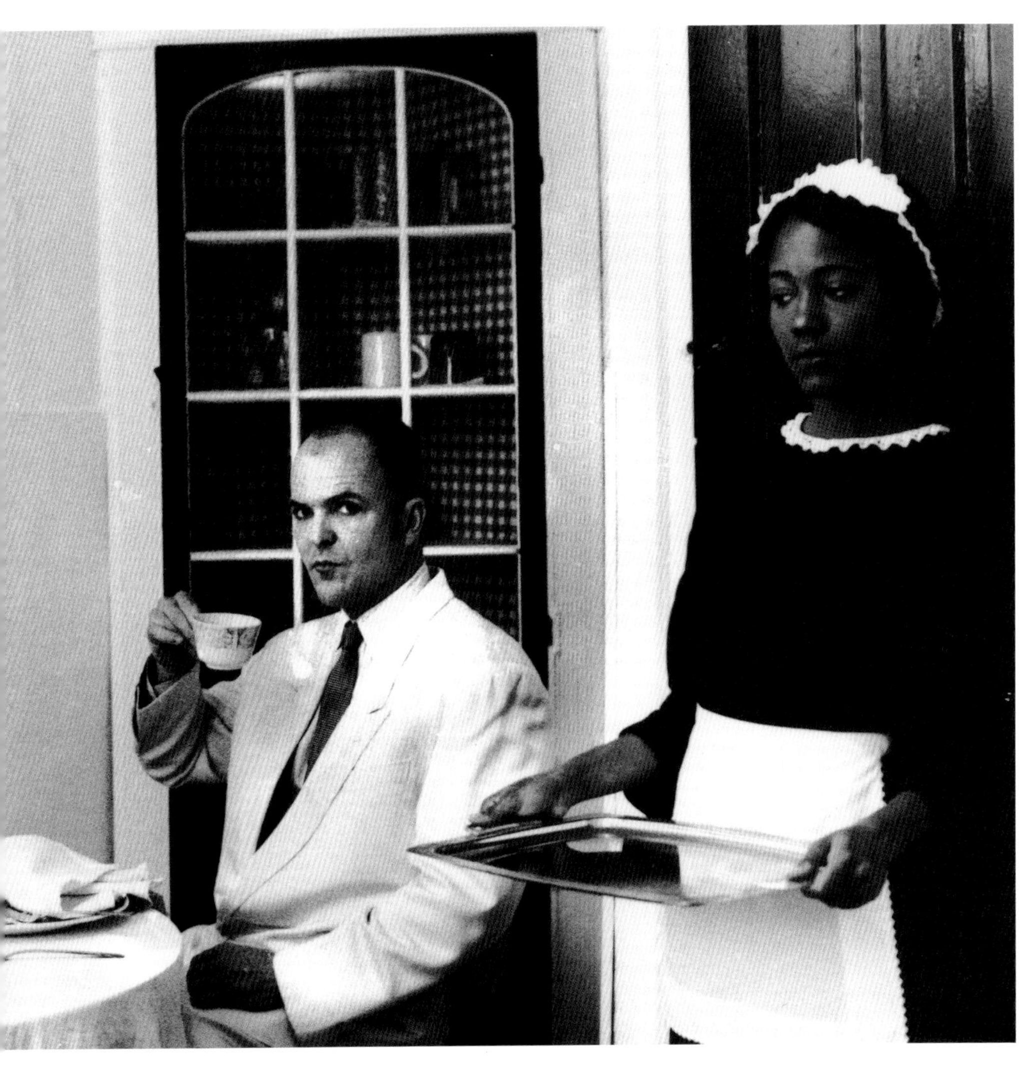

"MR. OWENS MEETS HIS MATCH", A SILVERSTAR PRODUCTION. 1937. STARRING THORNTON VAN CLYDE AS MR. OWENS AND LESLIE RANDALL AS MISS KATY BURKE. FEATURING FAY RICHARDS AS THE MAID.

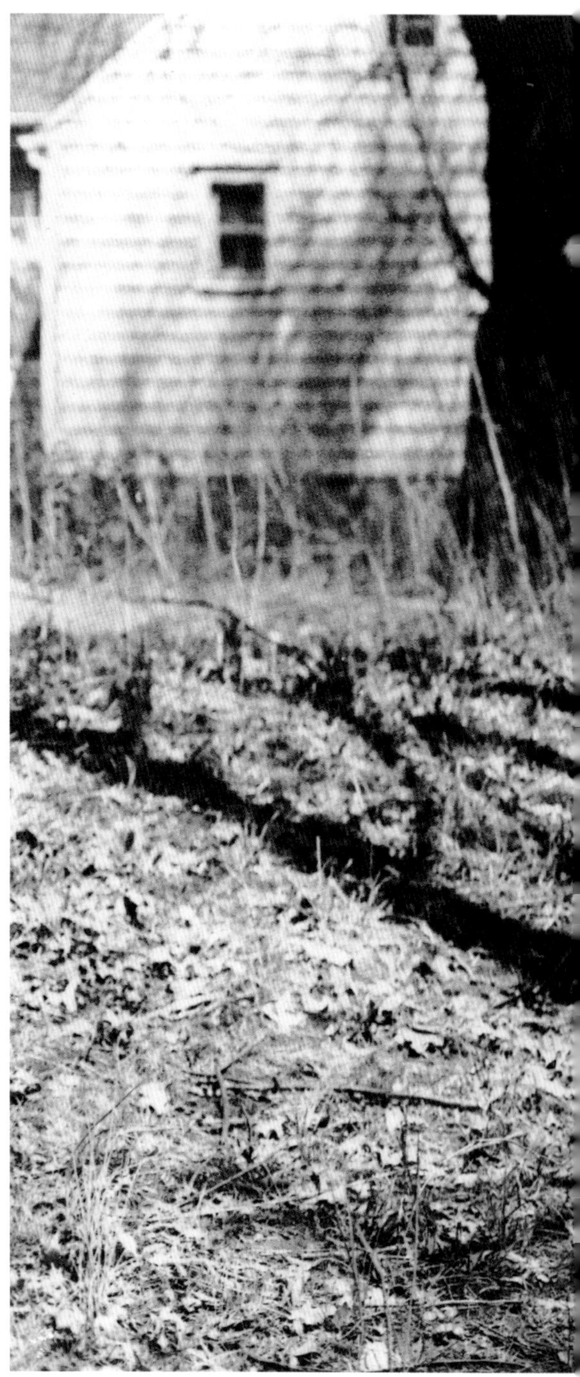

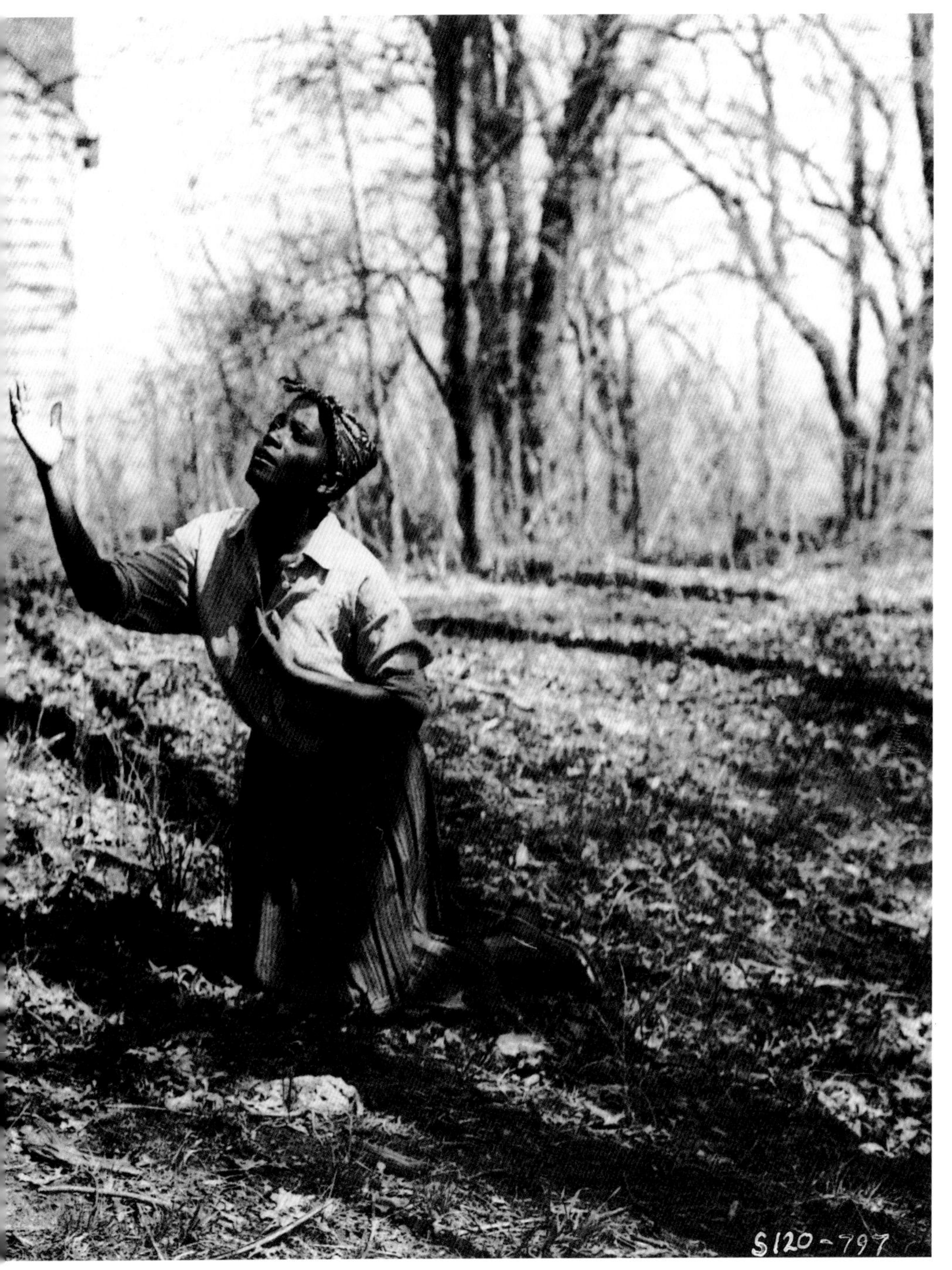
S120-797

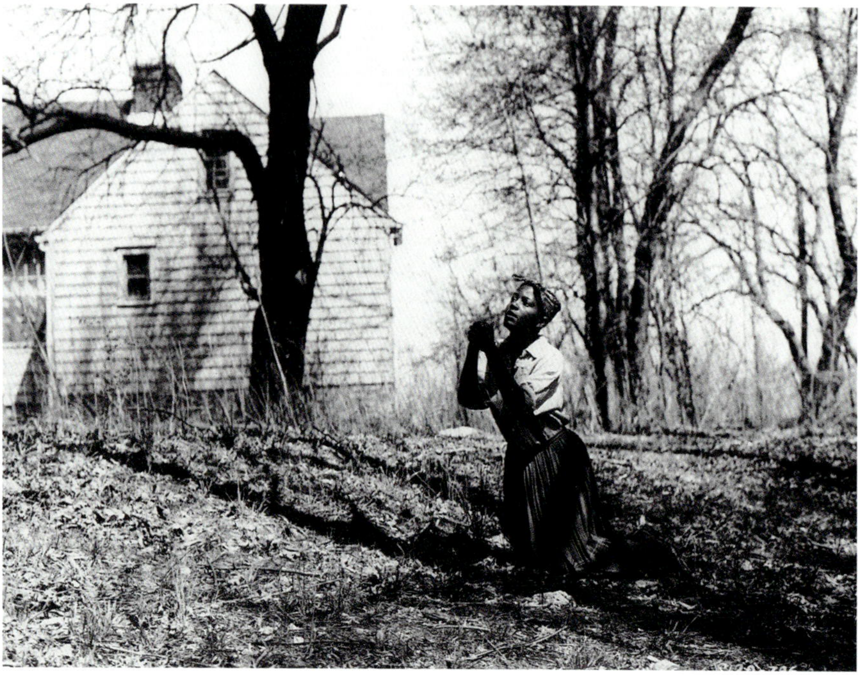

38

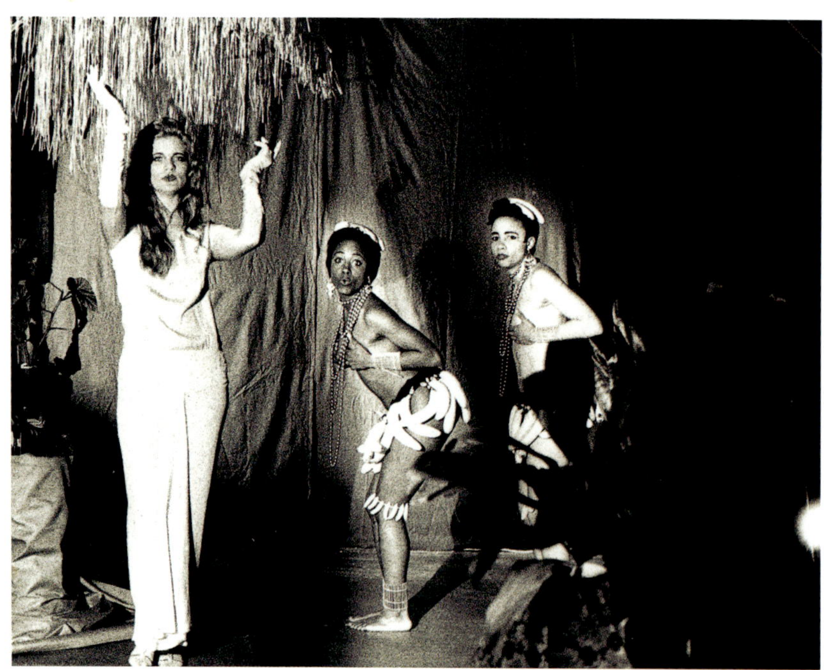

39

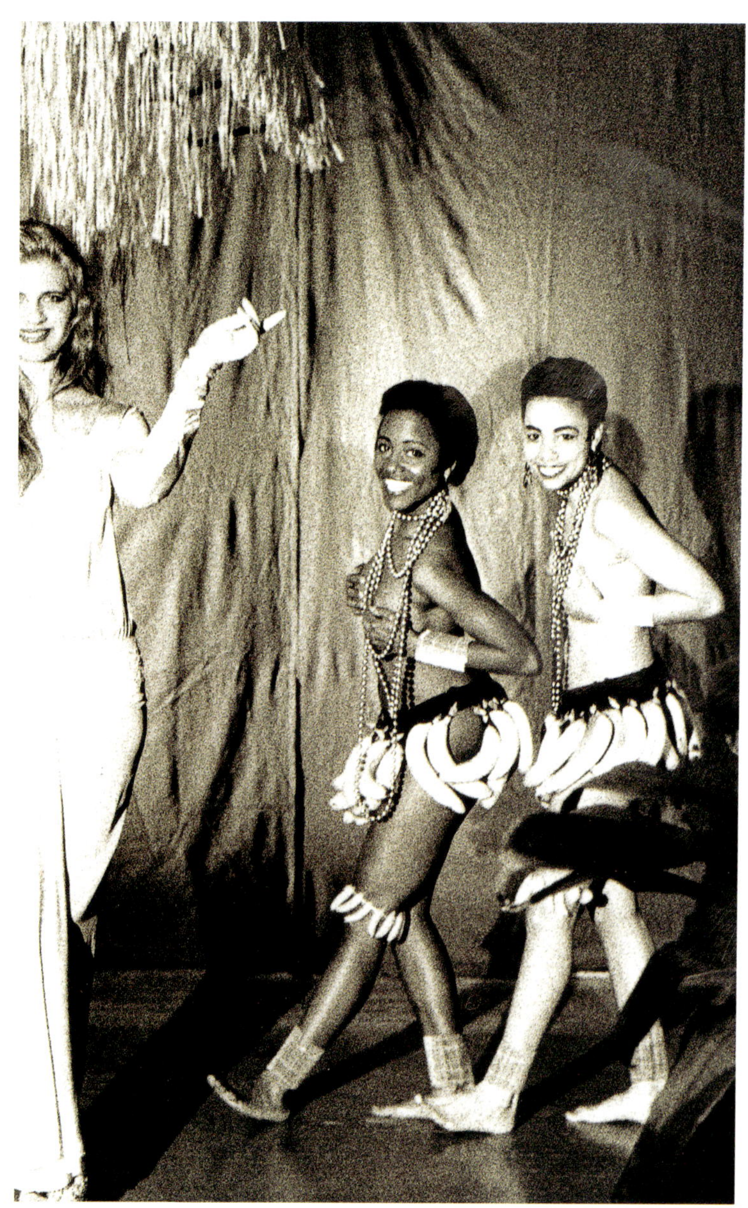

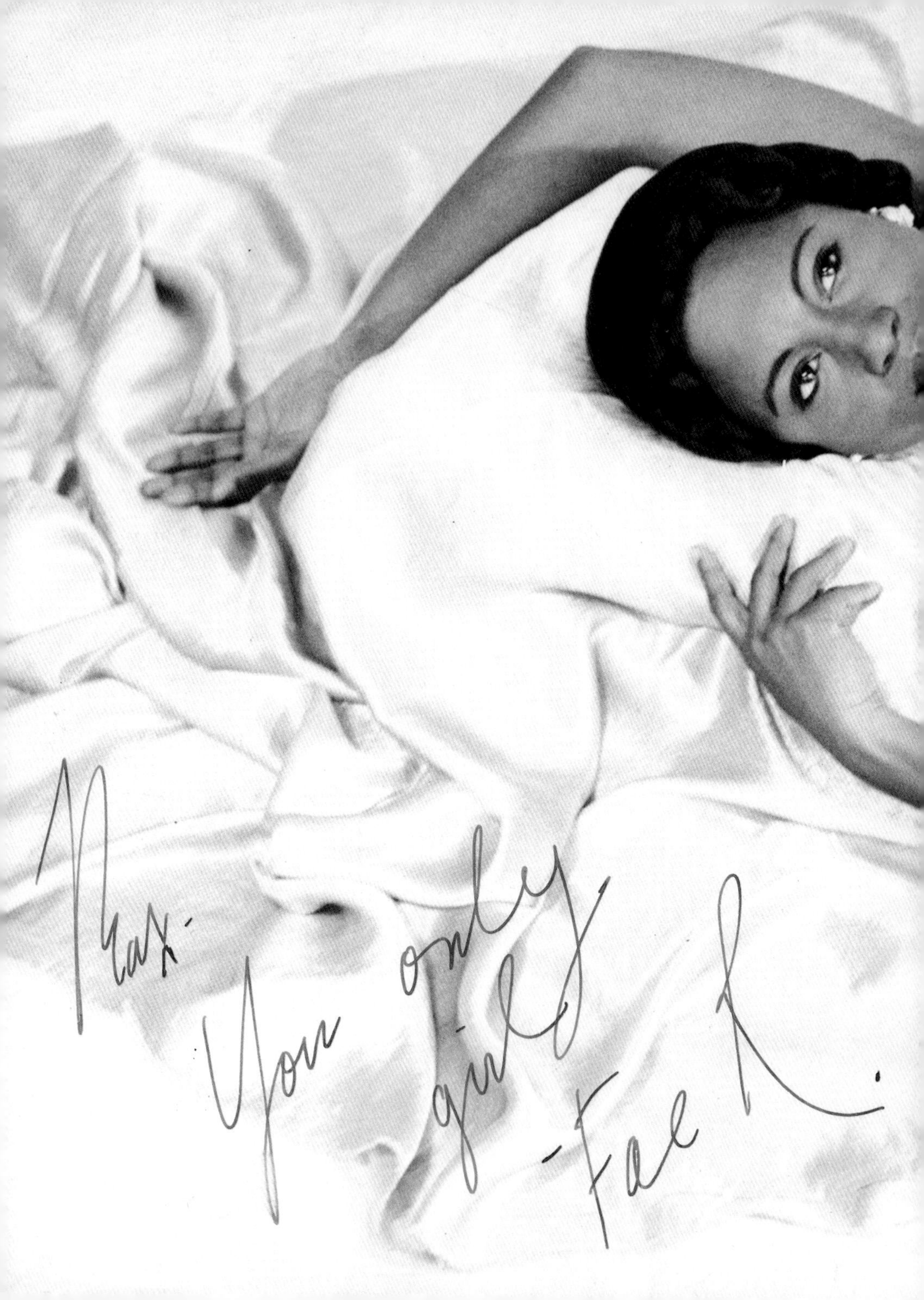
Max-
You only
girl
-Fae R.

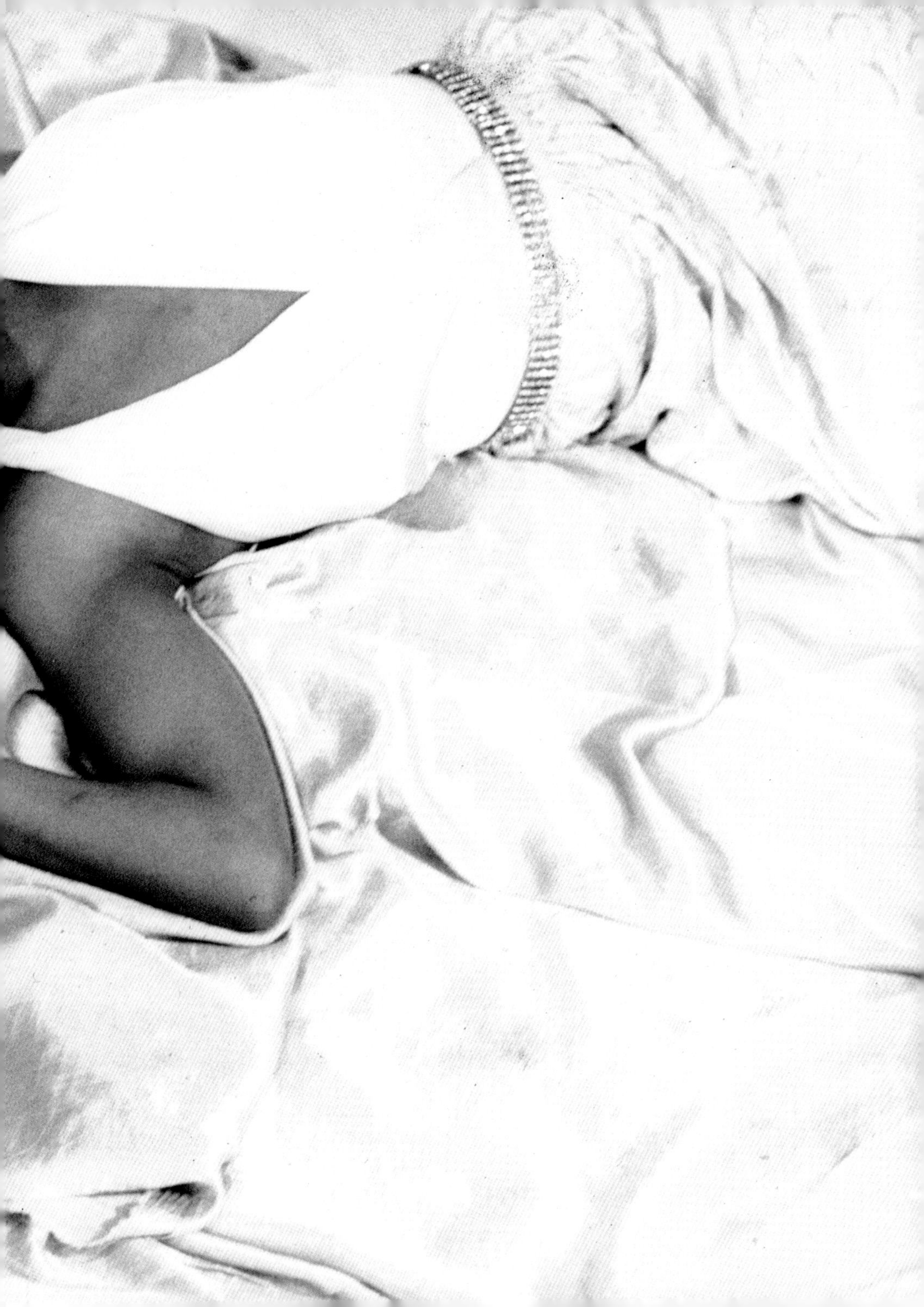

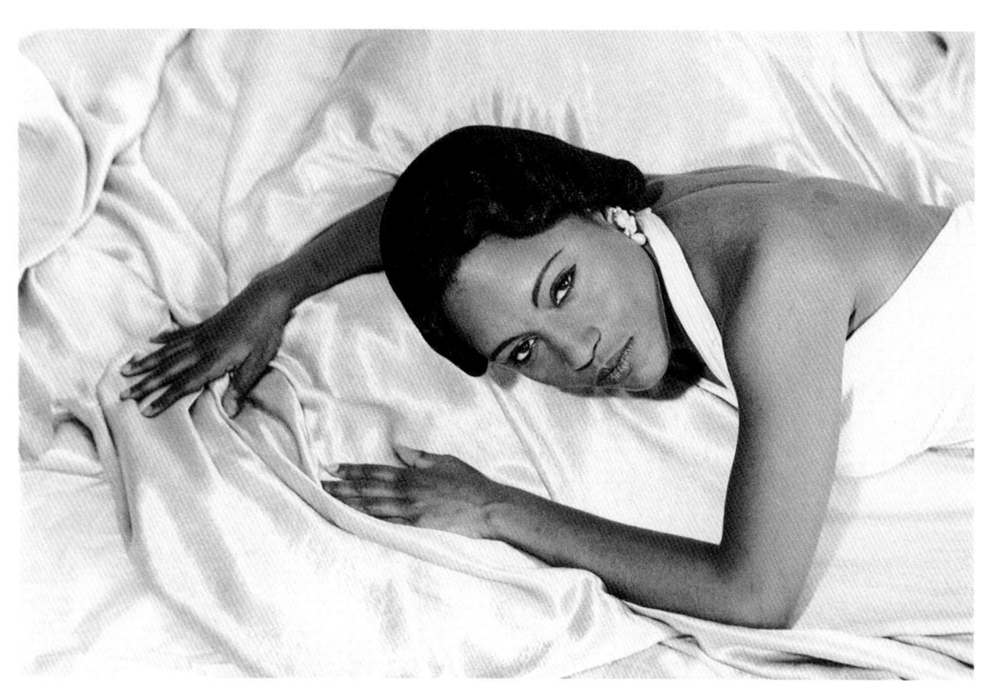

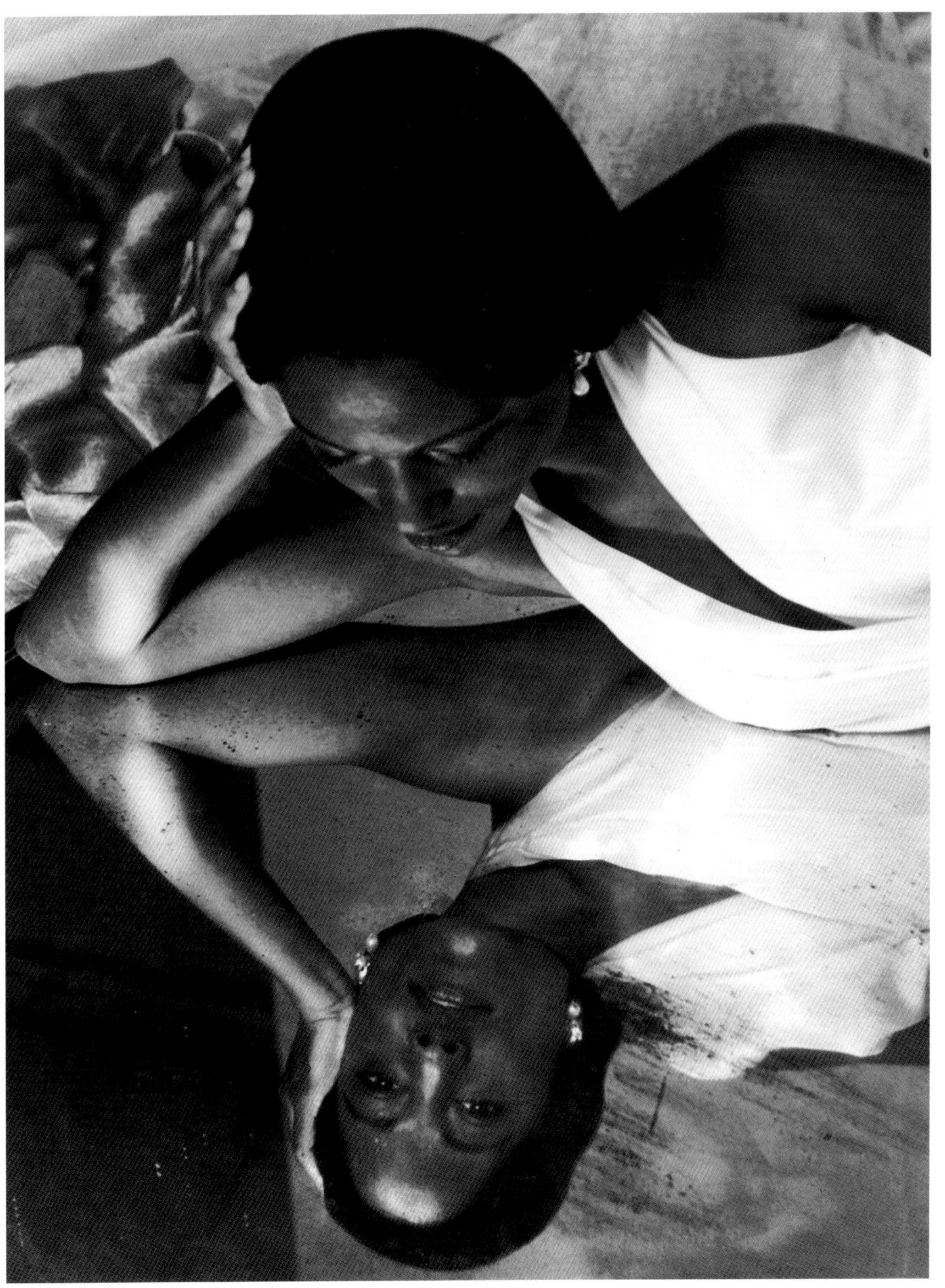

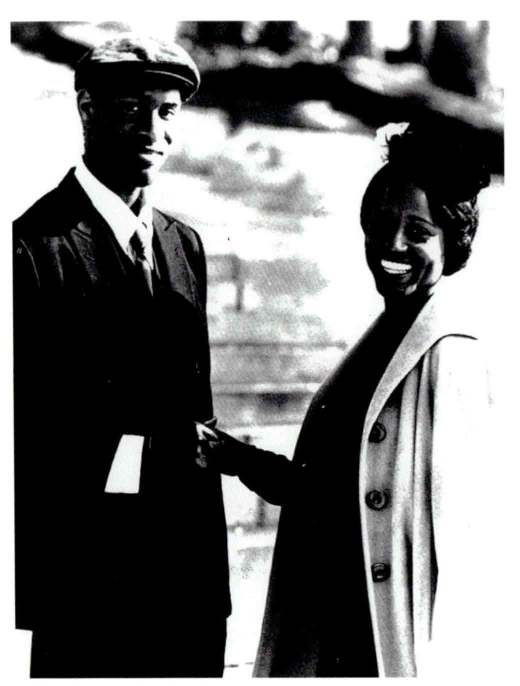

44

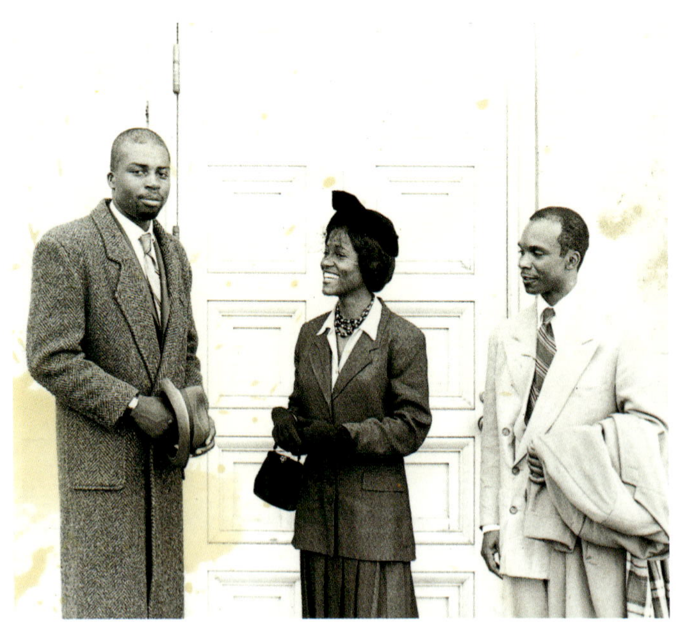

45

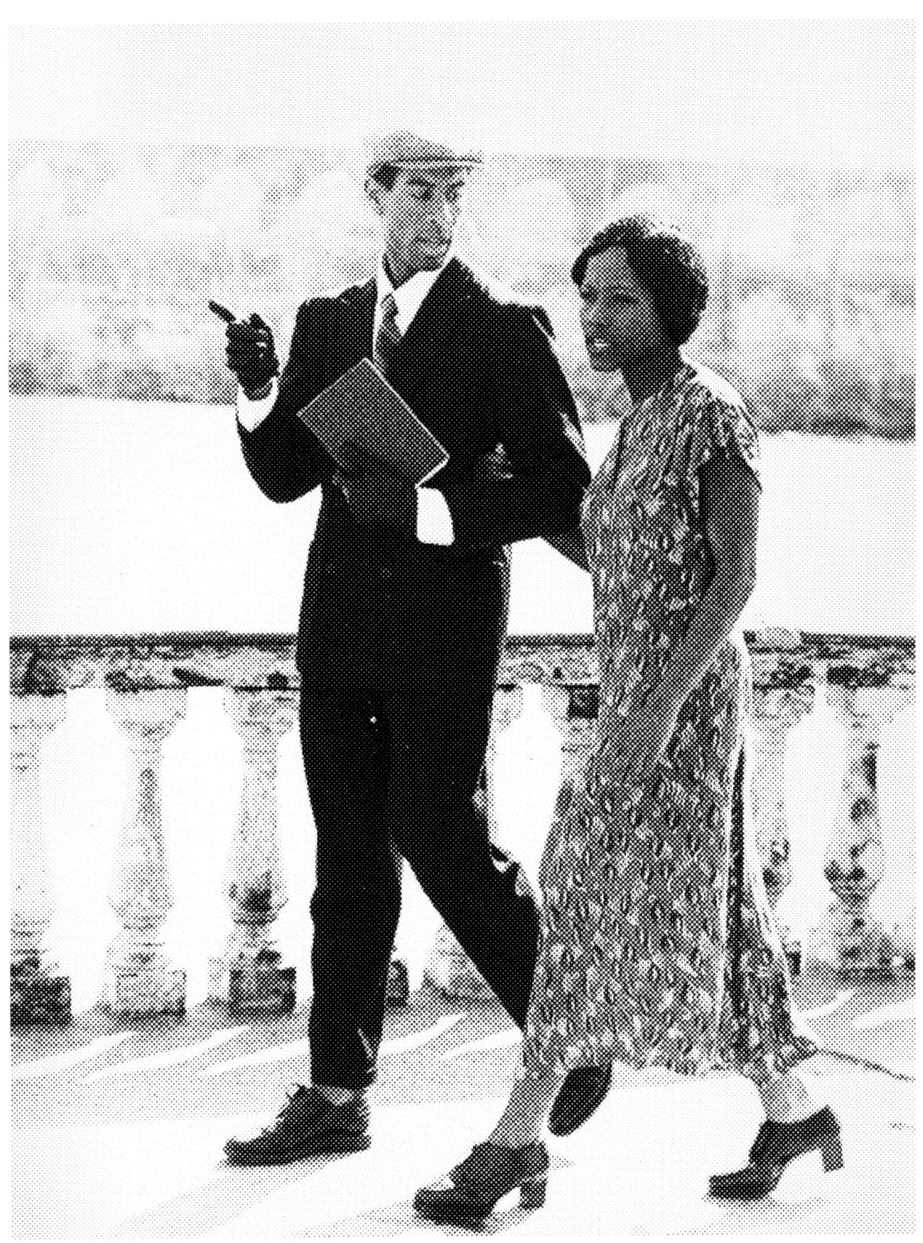

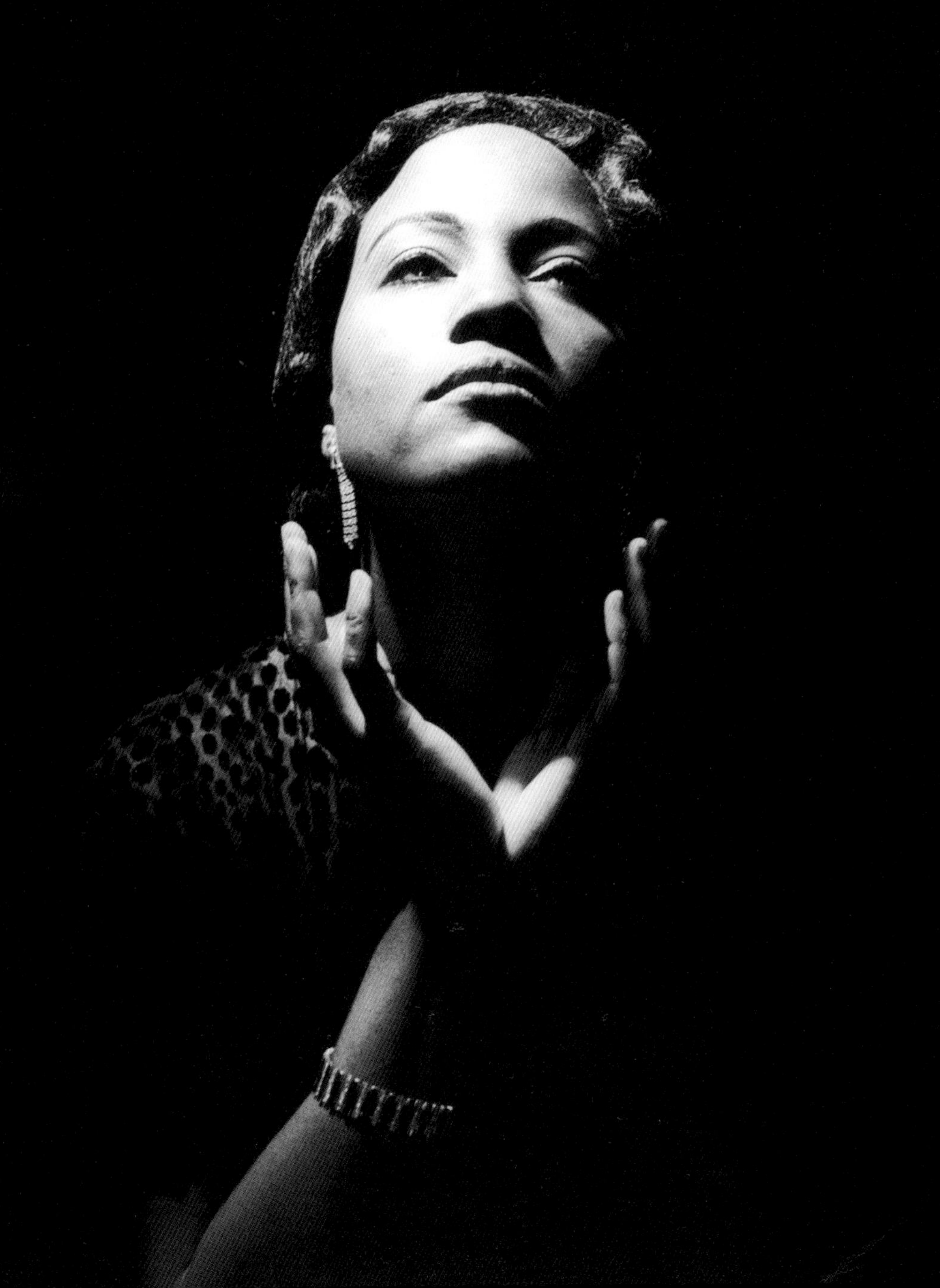

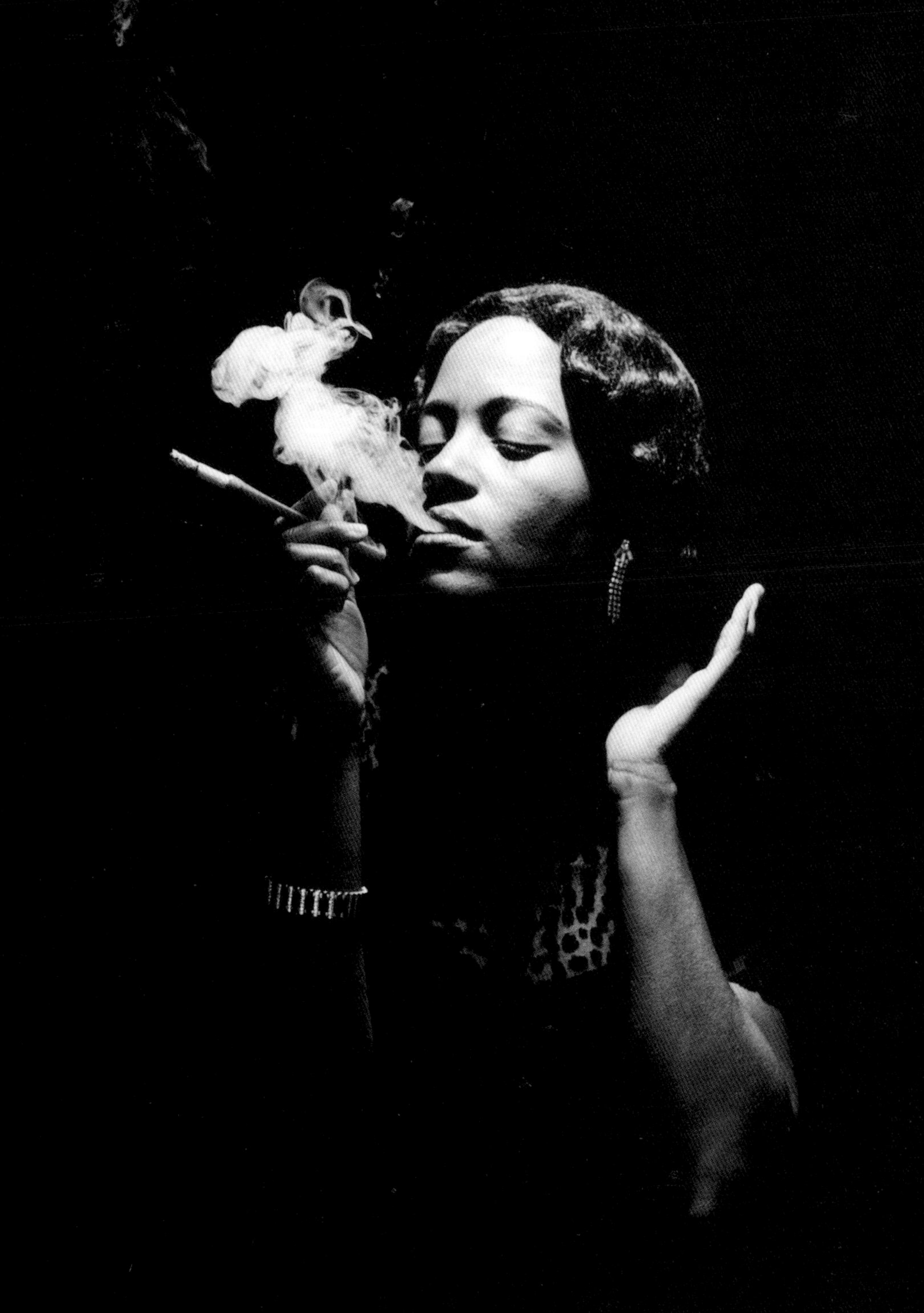

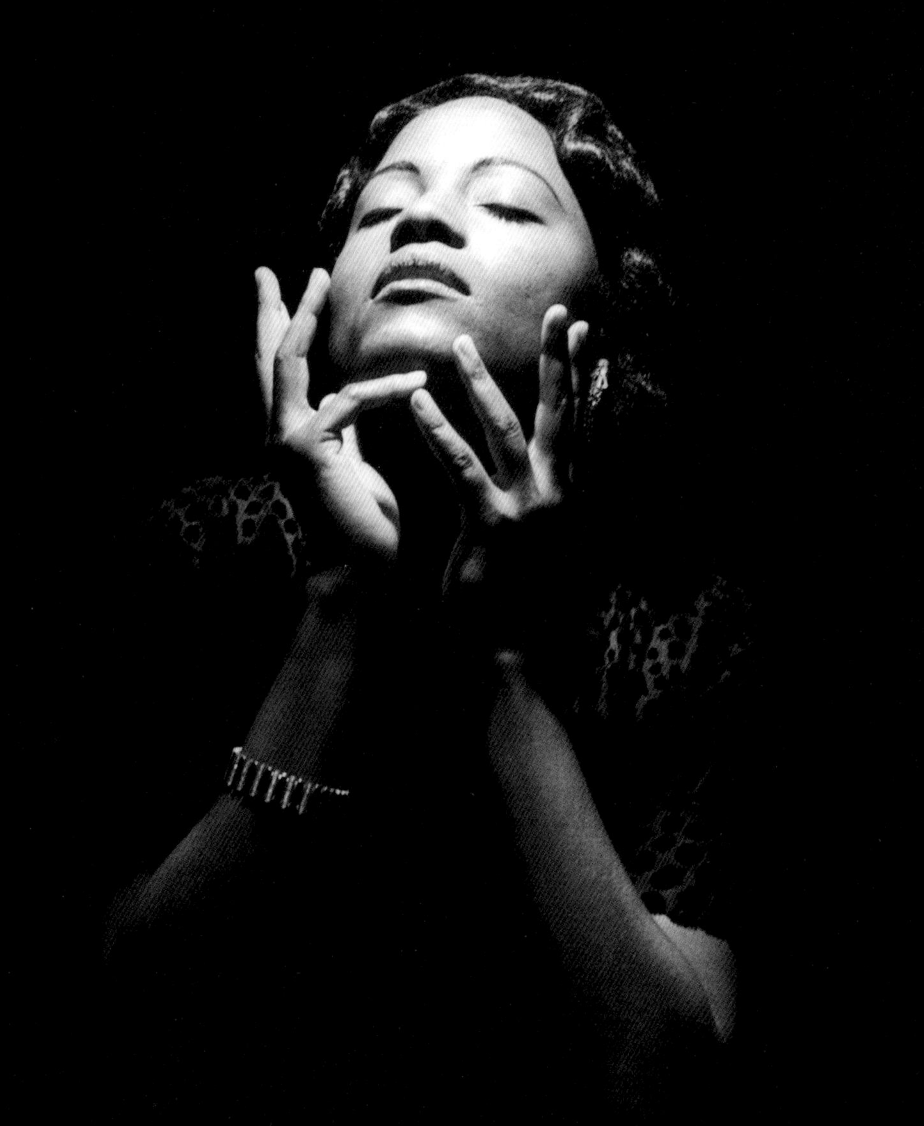

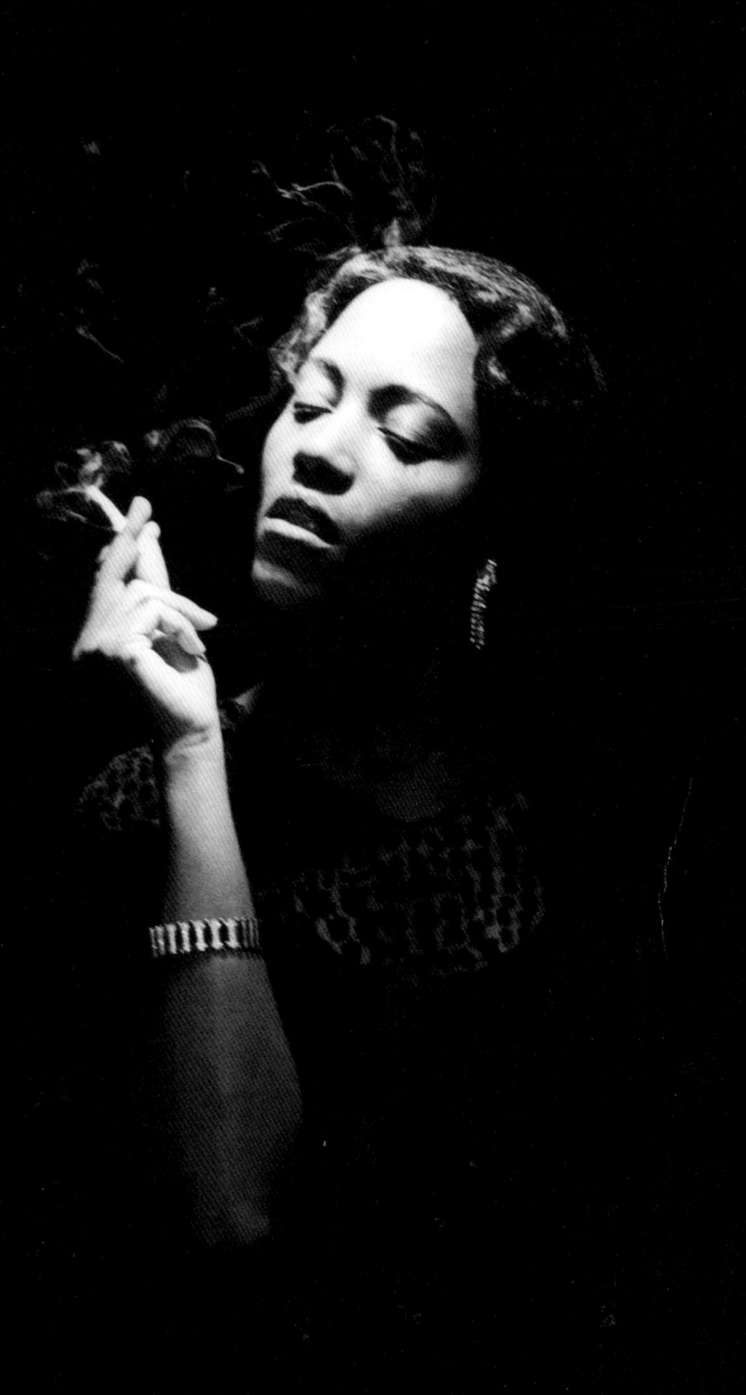

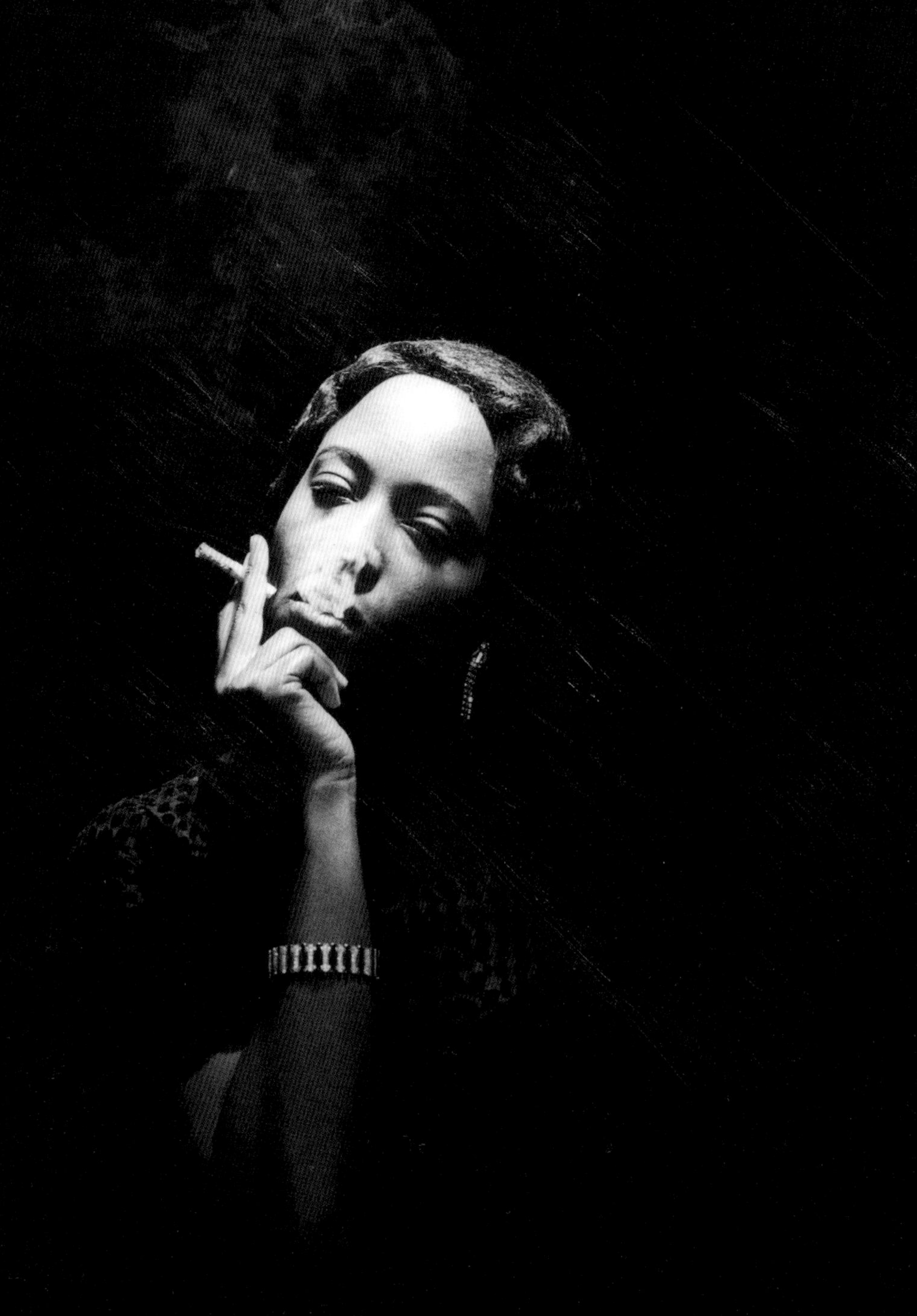

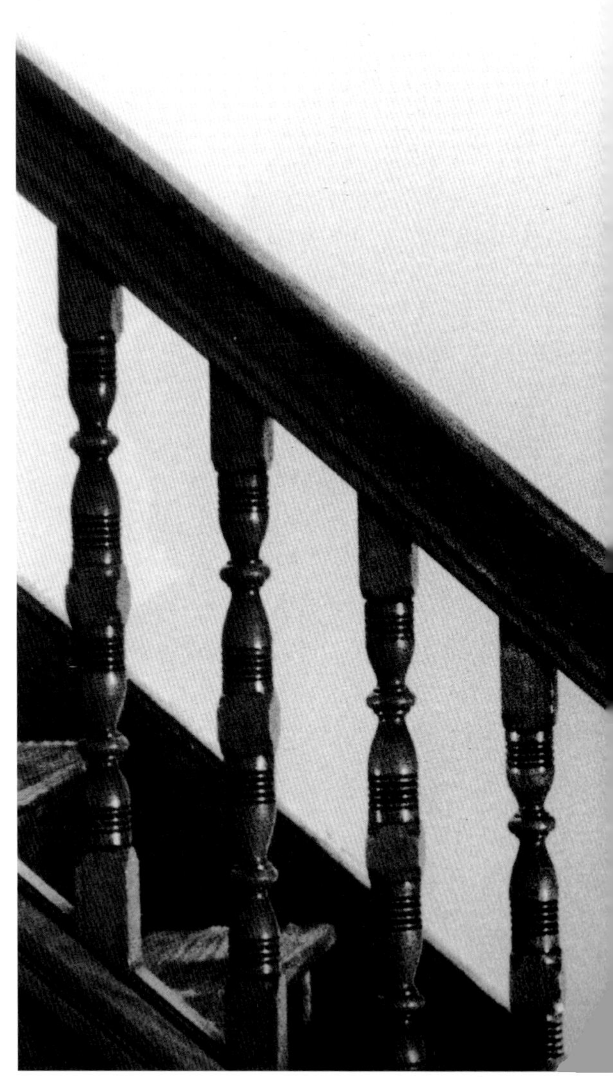

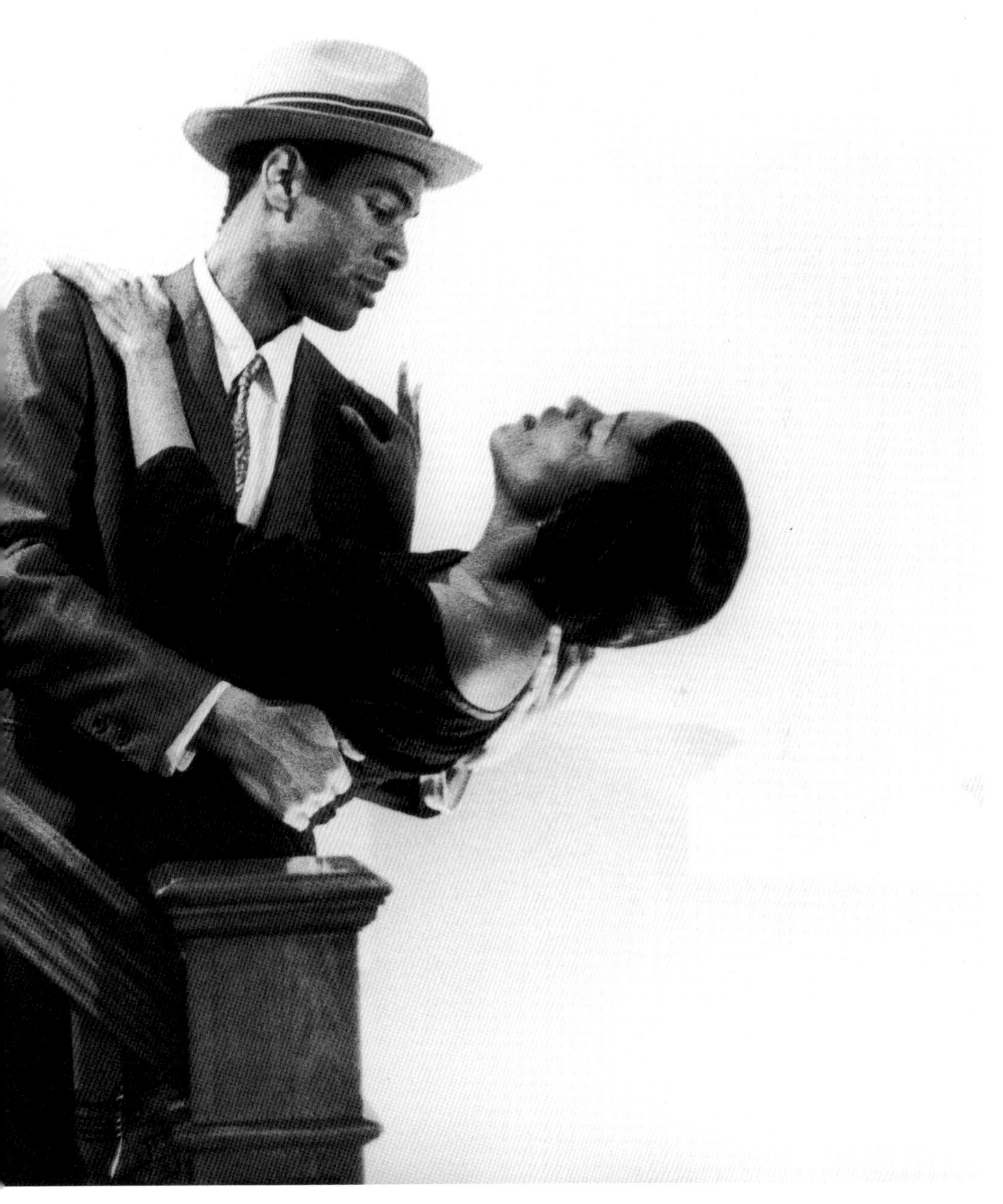

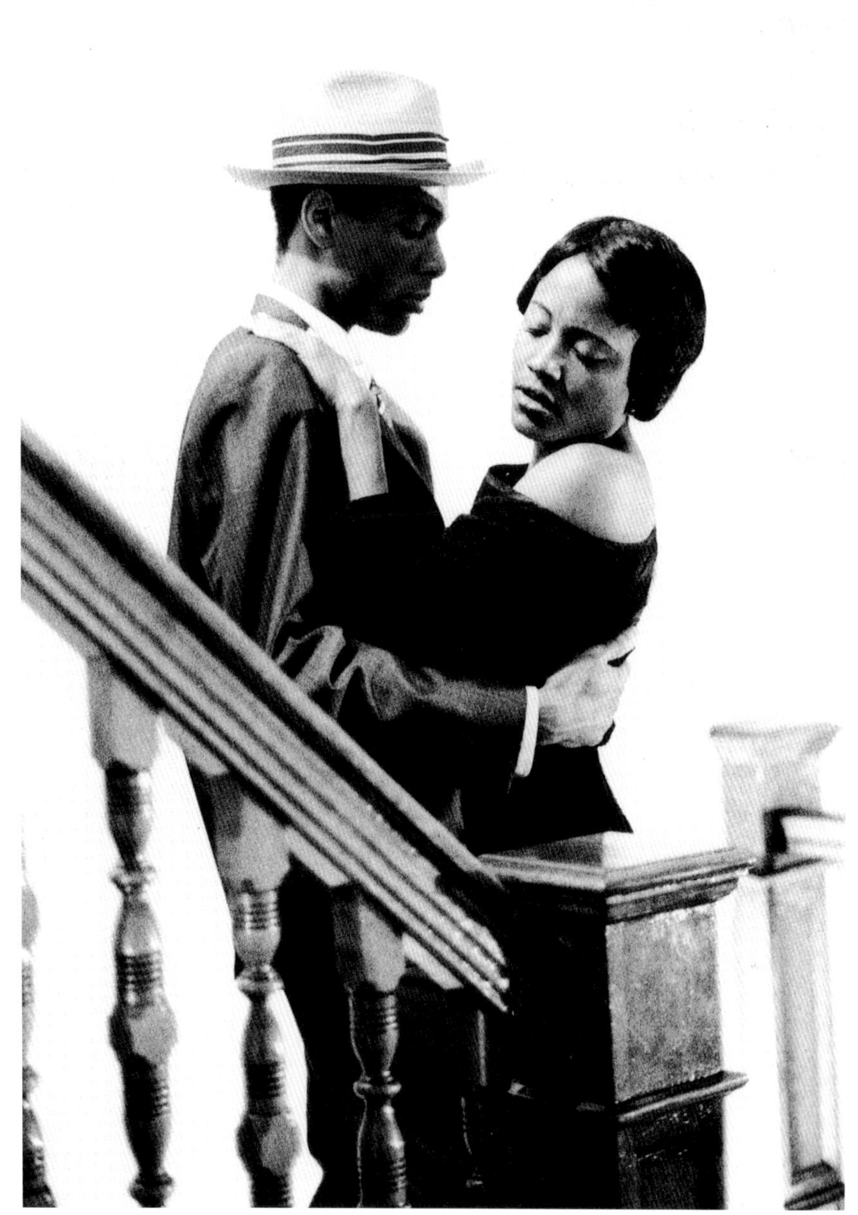

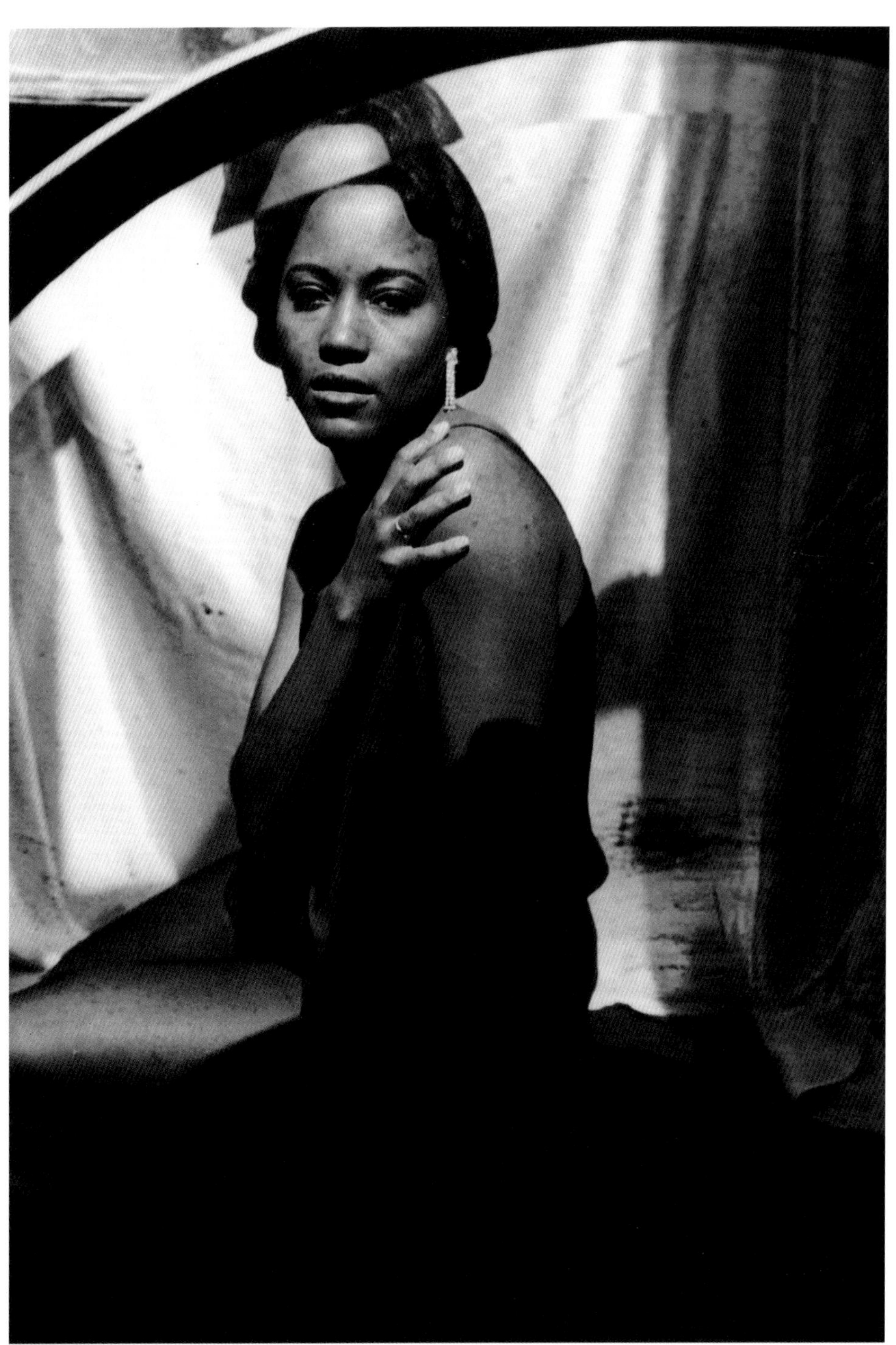

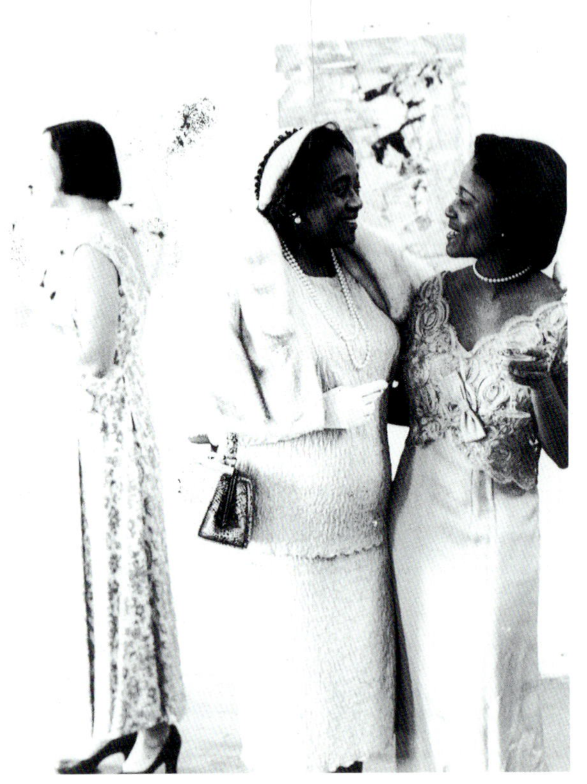

55

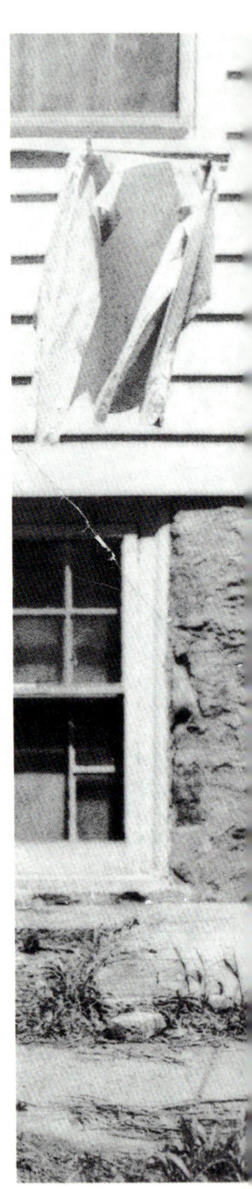

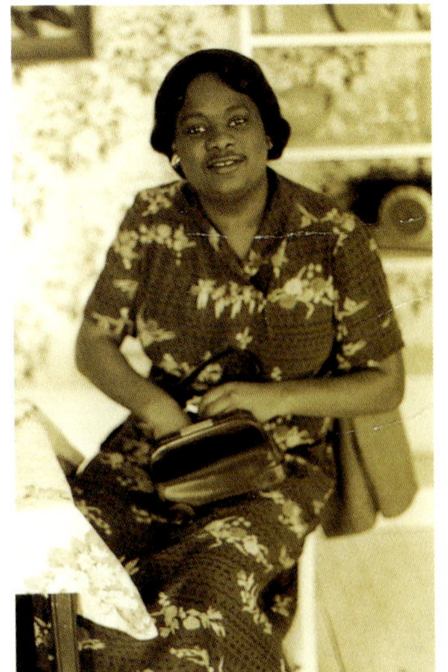

56

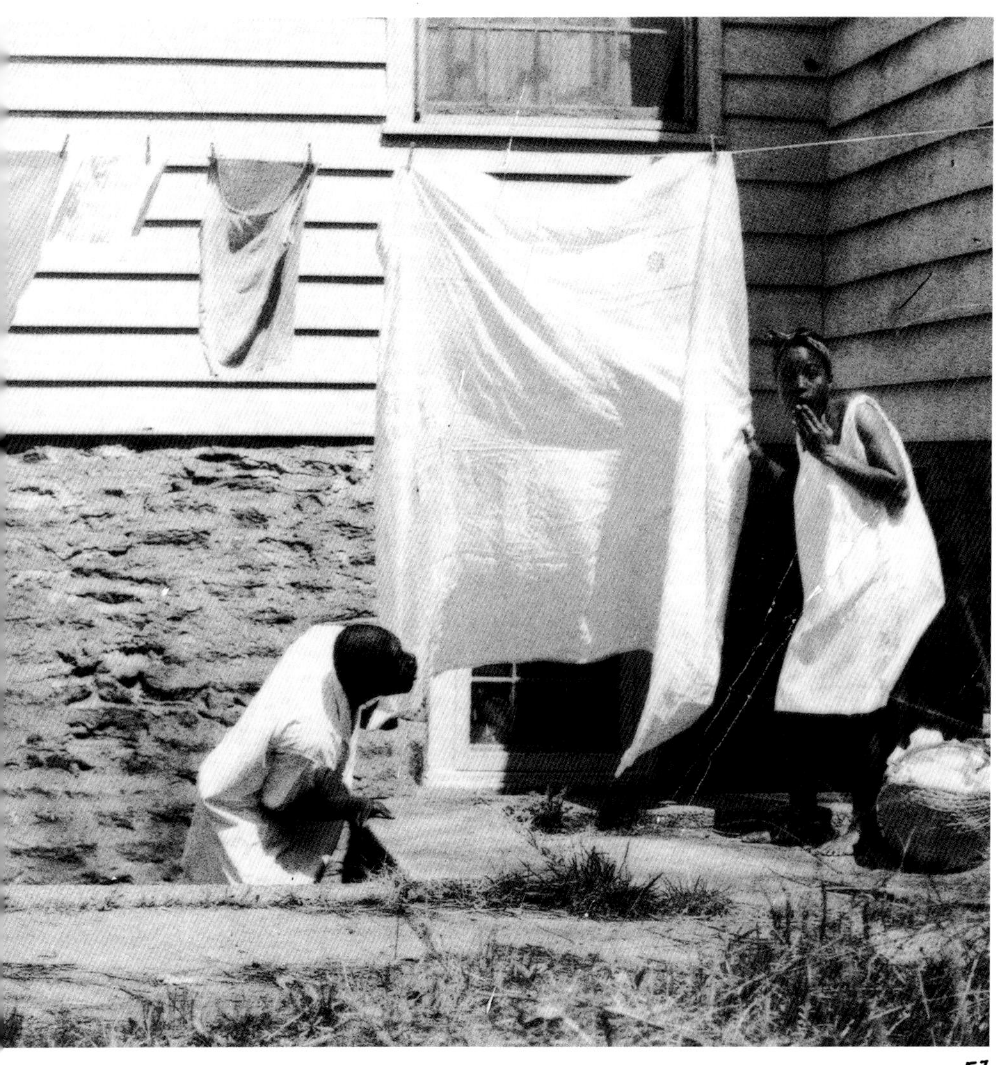

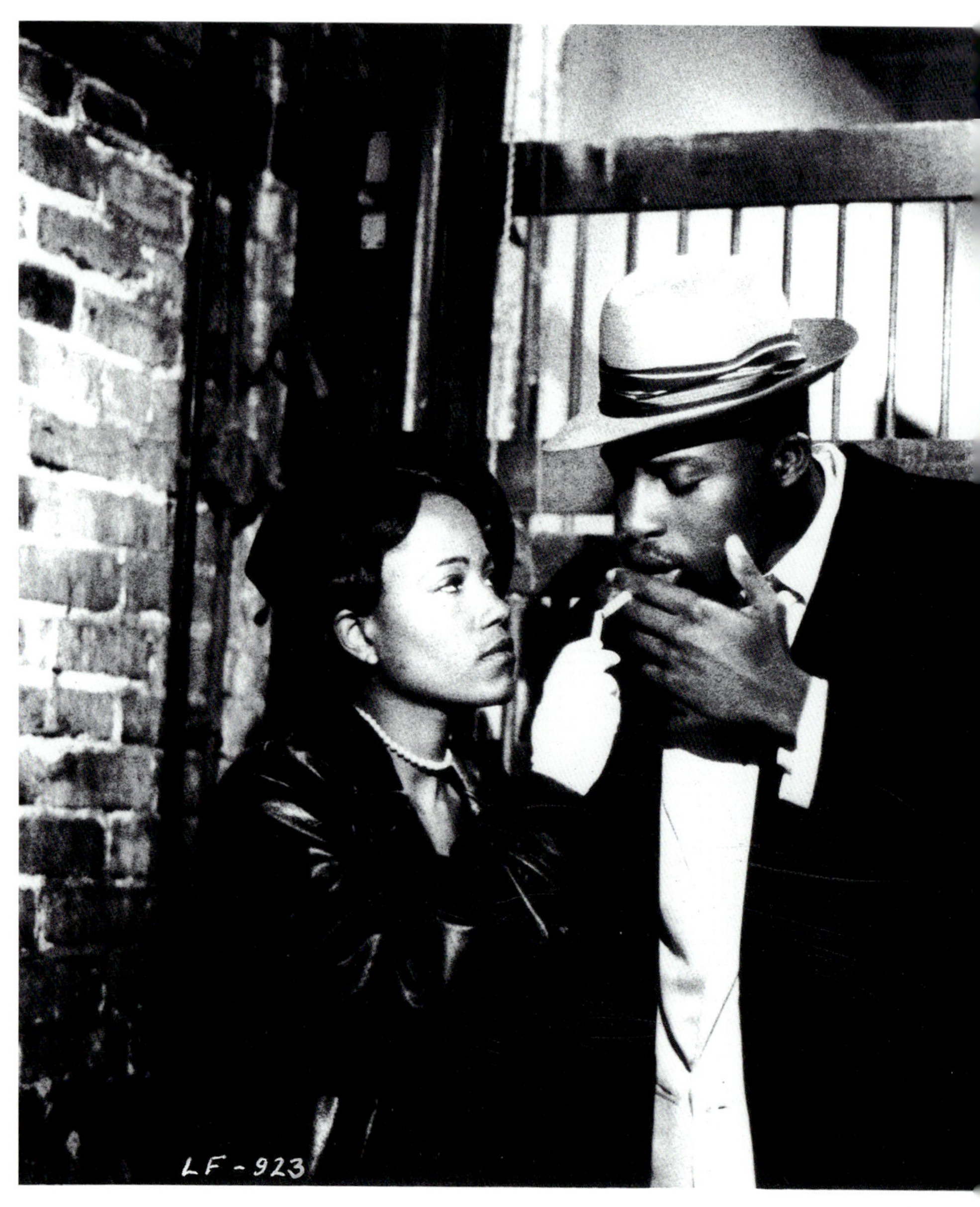

Black Guns. A Liberty Pictures release. Starring Fae
1941.

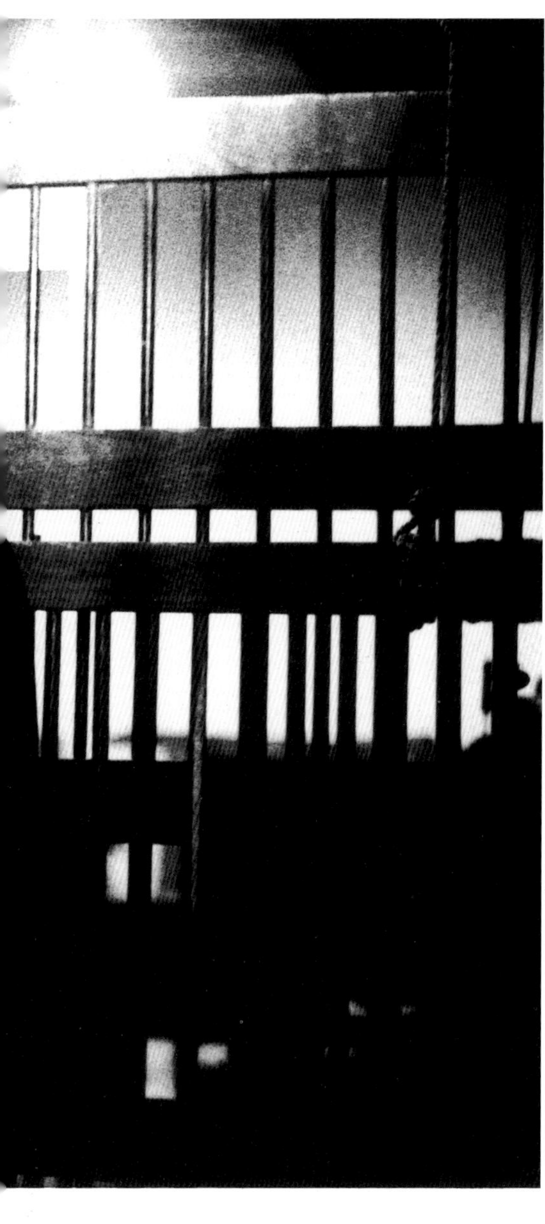

rds and Ray Blake.

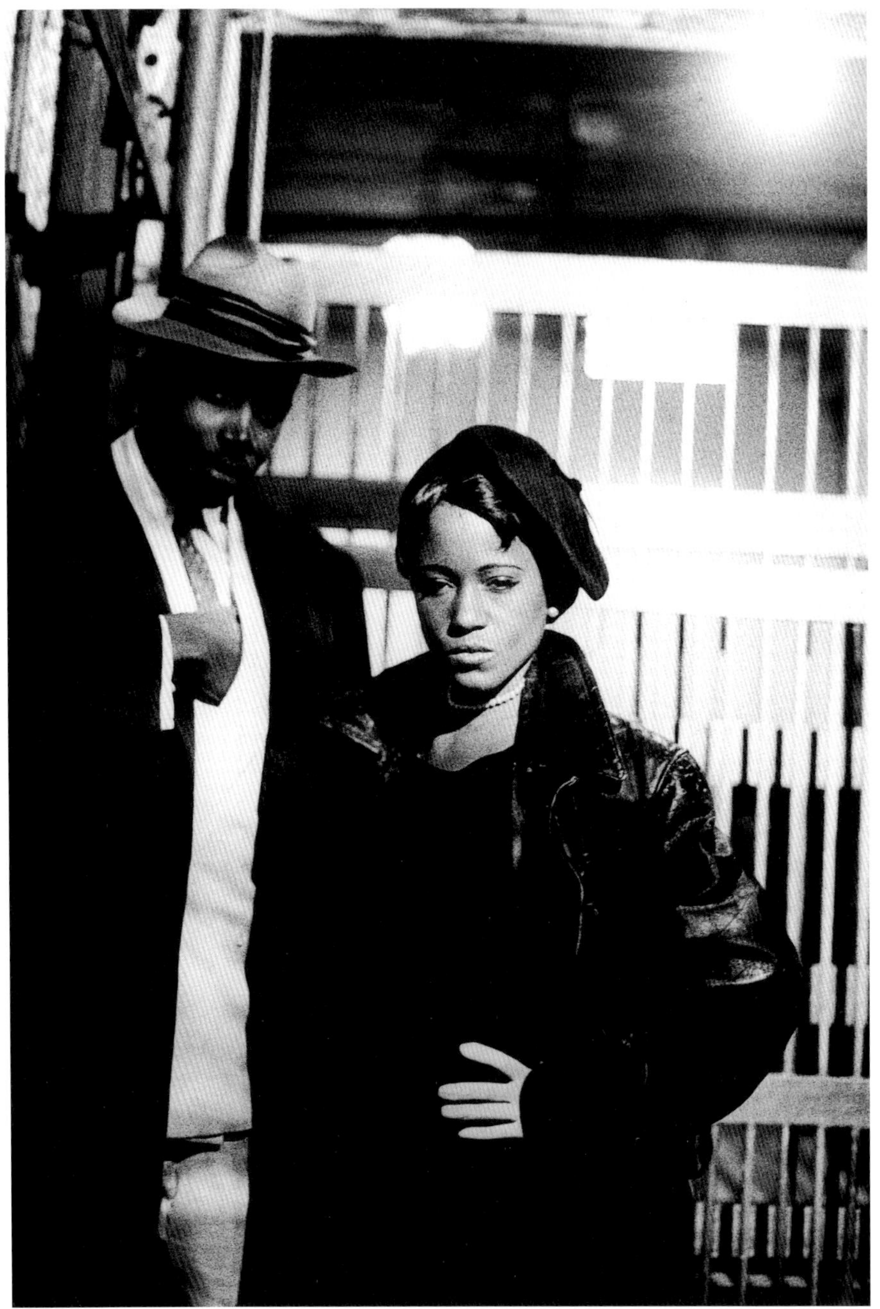

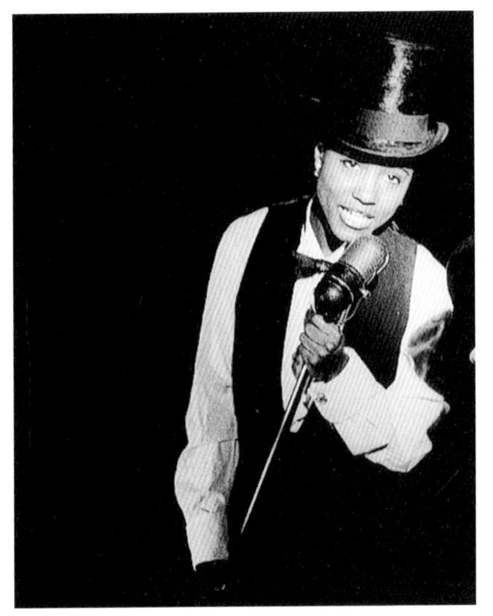

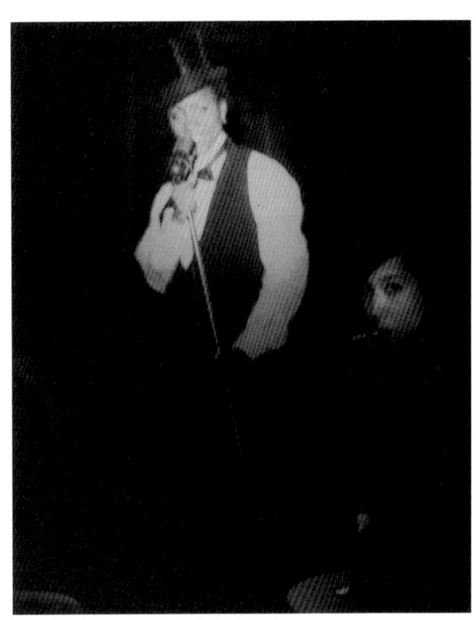

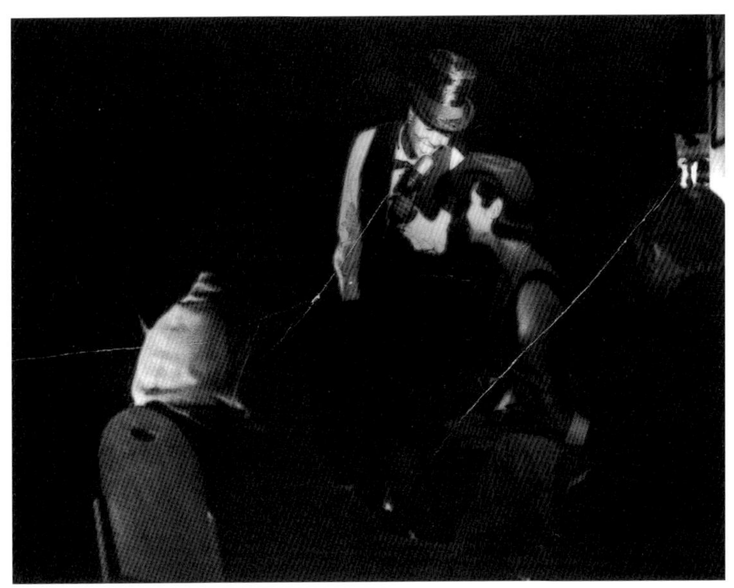

60-62

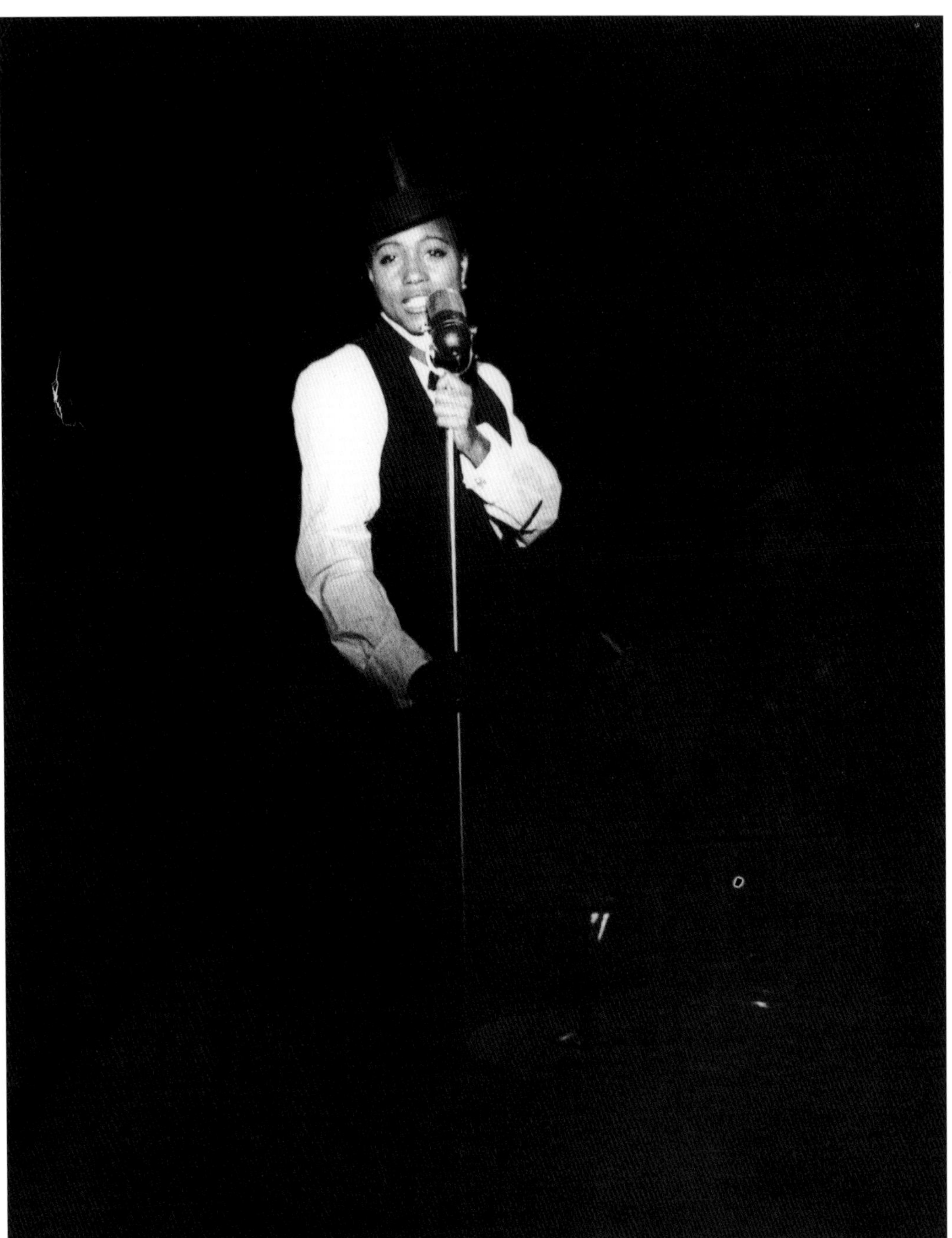

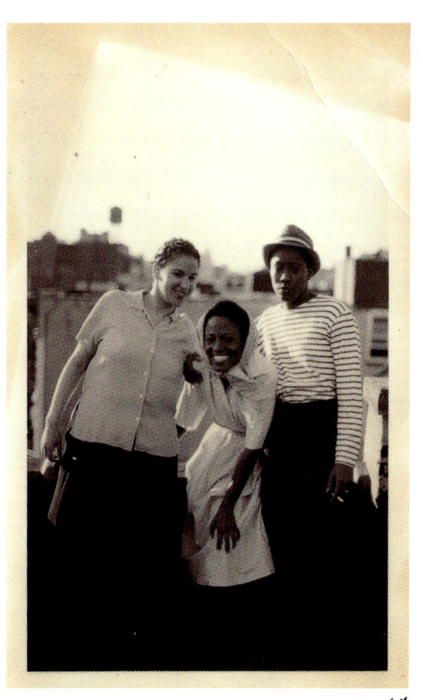

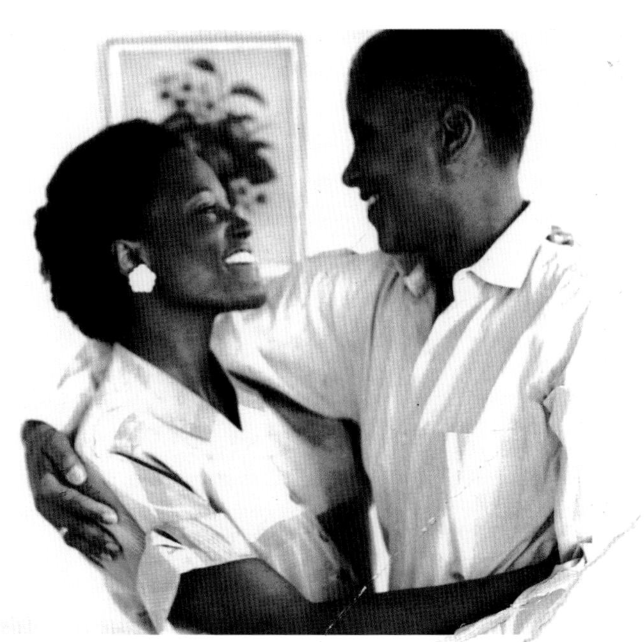

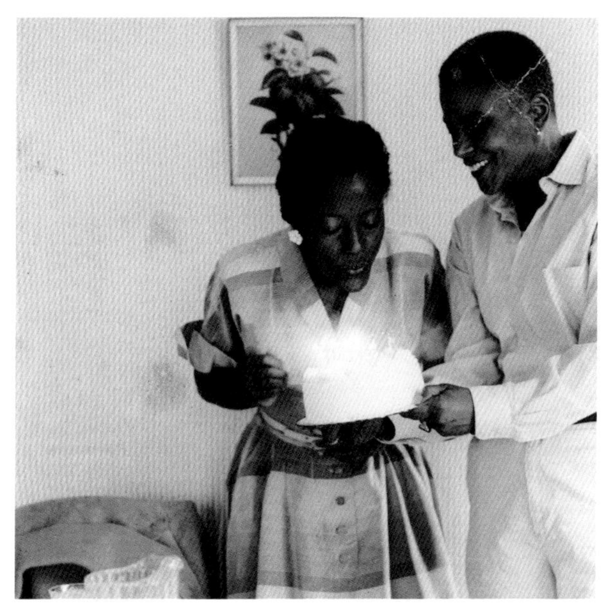

65 - 67

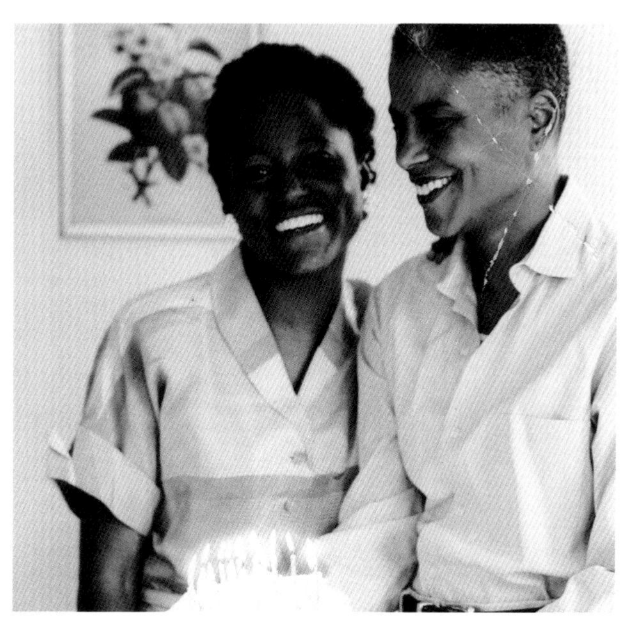

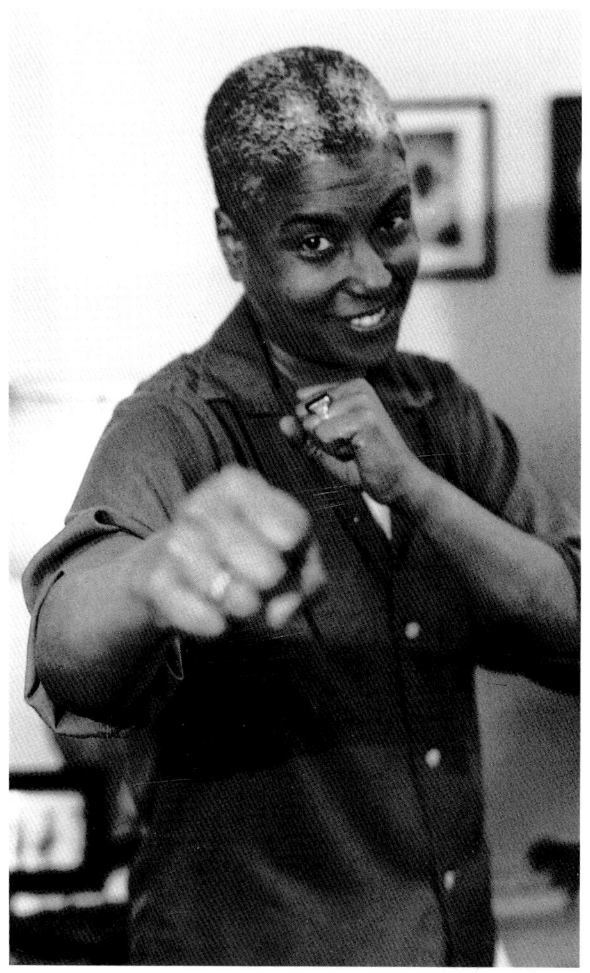

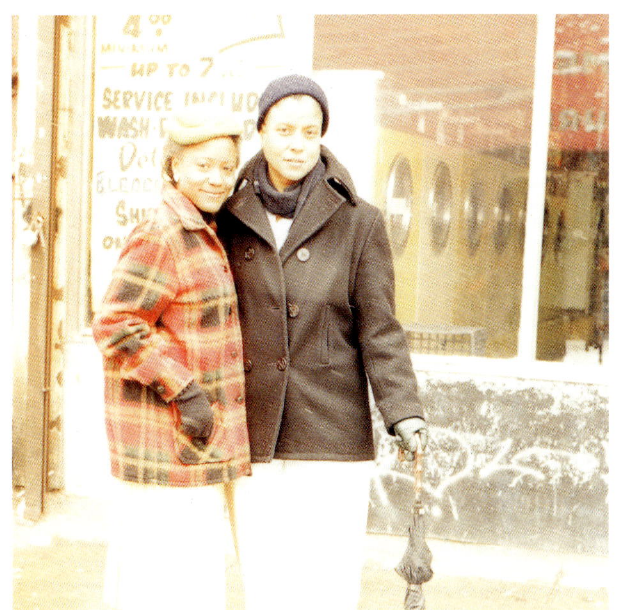

69

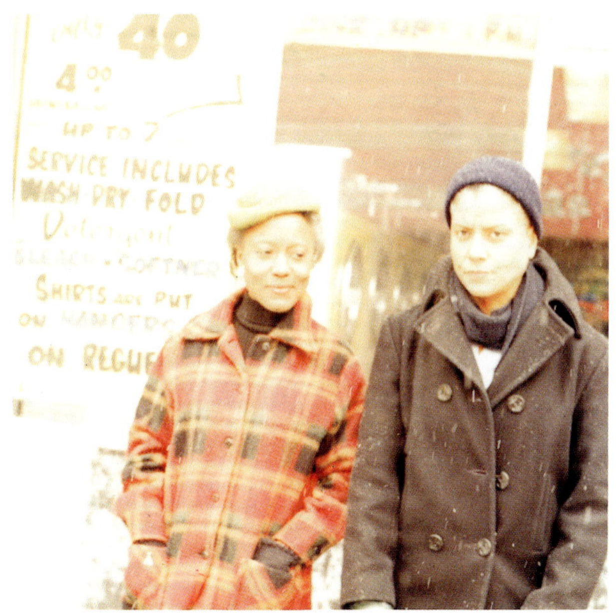

70

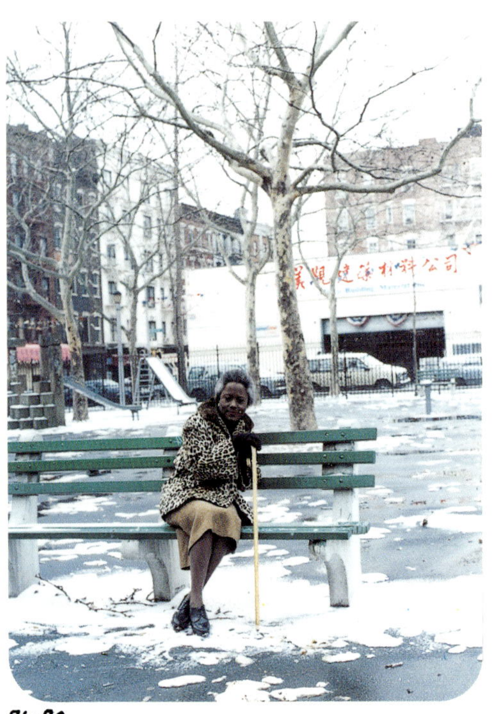

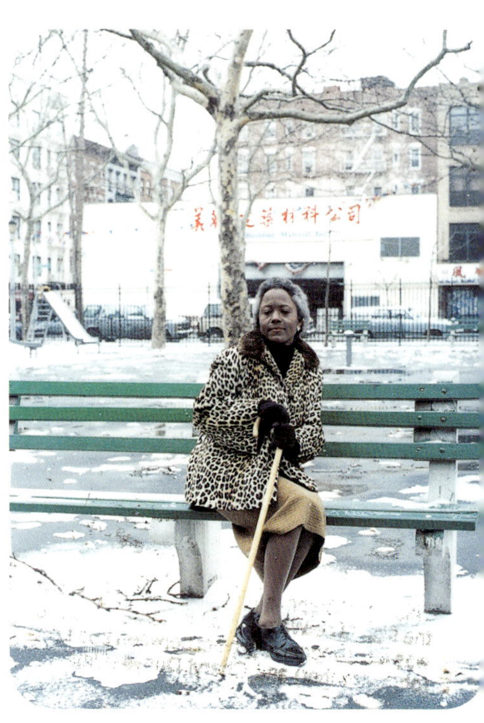

71 + 72

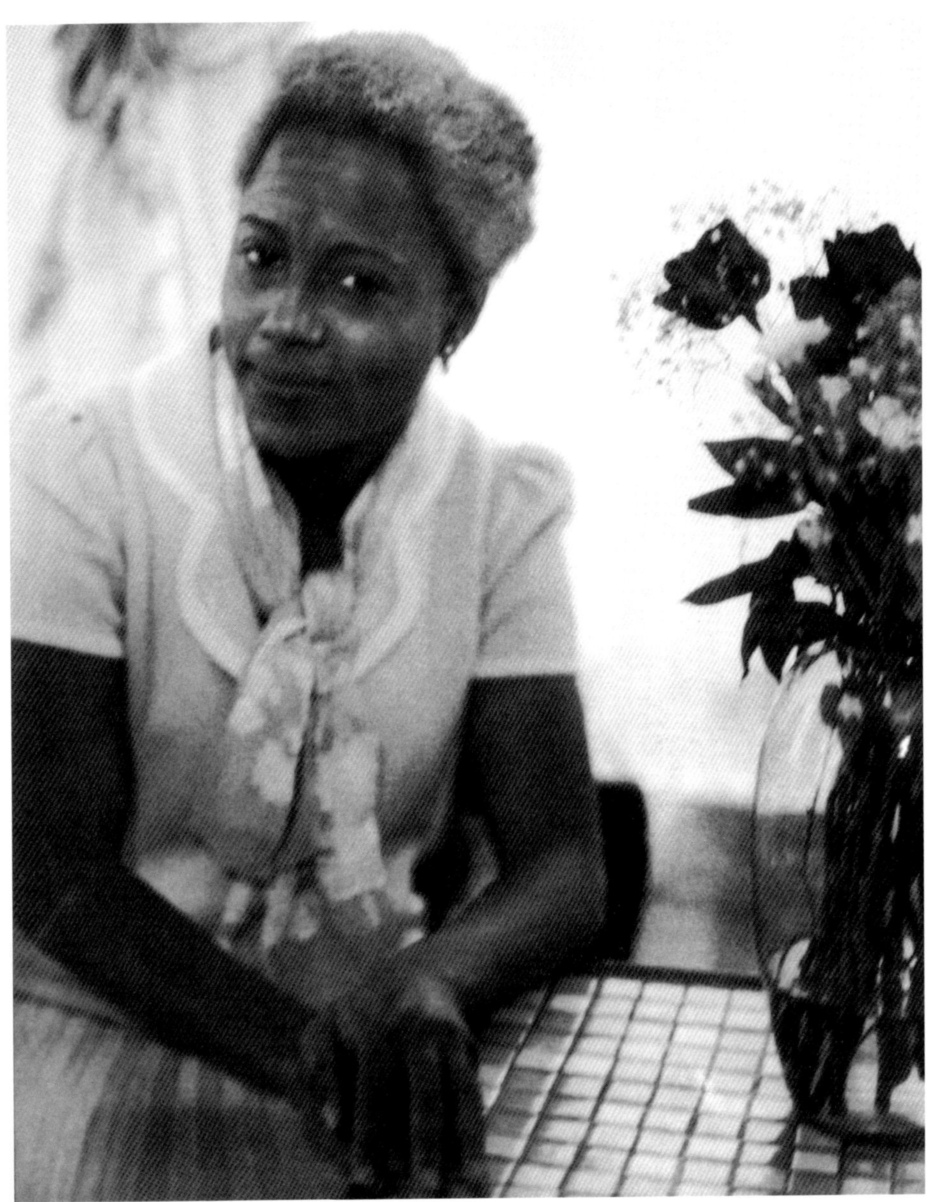

List of Photographs

1.&2. Reba Richardson, Fae's little sister.1924. Photo portrait by Cohen Bros. Photo Palace, Philadelphia. Fae Richards was born Faith Richardson, and later shortened her name.

3.Fred DeShields, Strawberry Mansion Bridge,Philadelphia.1925. Fae's lifelong friend. As children, Faith and Fred often sang together on the street for change, billing themselves as a "brother and sister" act.

4.Oscar Williams and Fae Richards. Philadelphia. Date unkown. (early 1920's). Williams was a jazz drummer from North Philly. He got Fae her first radio spot-on the Beechy Beechum Contest-with a ditty he wrote and she sang. Some say they were married for a time, even that they had a child together. Others claim Fae rejected his marriage proposal and that he drank himself to death over her.

5.Oscar, with Fae's dog,Frankie. Fairmont Park.Philadelphia1923.

6.The Van Clyde family (Edward,Irene,Catherine,Eleanor,&Parker). 1928. Fae worked as a servant for the VanClyde's for several years- at least from 1926-1931.

7.Eleanor VanClyde with a guest.(pomssibly Margaret Fitzgerald). 1930. Fae can be seen in the background.

8.Martha Page and Catherine VanClyde.1930. This picture was probably taken by Thornton VanClyde(Edward's brother). Thornton, an actor, was fx friends with Martha Page in the beginning of her career. It was through this friendship that Fae Richards and Martha Page first met. When a bit player backed out of a small, non-speaking pxxrole in "Jersey Girl", Miss Page cast Miss Richards in the part of'the maid'. It was Fae's first appearance on film.

9. Fae Richards. Winner of the Beechy Beechum Bicarbonate Jingle Contest. 1923 or 24.

10.Martha Page on the set of "Jersey Girl".1931. Newark Studios.

11.Martha Page at Newark Studios. Photographed for the story 'The Girl Director of "Jersey Girl"' in The Philadelphia Inquirer. October,1931.

12.&13.Fae Richards and friends. Josie,Bobbi,and unidentified man. June 1926.

14.Martha Page at Newark Studios.Early 1930's.

15.Sandra Vincent and Fae Richards in "Jersey Girl".Newark Studios. 1931.

16.&17.Fae Richards and Martha Page. Garden State Park. 1933. These two pictures are the earlies t rec or d of Richard's and Pa ge's off-screen r elationship.

18.Film still from "Louisiana Lady". Fae Richards and Hambone Jones. Newark Studi os.1933. This is Fae's first speaking role. The picture was a big box office sucess, Newark Studios largest-grossing pi cture to date. Based on it's success, Hollywood's Silverstar Studio offered both Martha Page and Fae Richards c ontracts. Miss Page signed a five-picture deal. The terms of Miss Ric hards contract are not known.

19.,20,21.,&22. Fae Richards, Martha Page and three unidentified friends at the Harlem Hotspot.1933.

23.M.Page and F.Richards at a Paramount Studio party for the premiere of "The Scarlet Empress", a 1934 film starring Marlene Dietr ich. (newsreel footage of this event also extant in the Ric hards arc hive.)

24.Martha Page at work. Silve rstar Studio. Hollywood,1934. photograph accompanied an article in 'Variety'.

25.&26.Martha Page and Fae Ric hards, at their home inx xxhxx the Hollywood Hills. Mid-1930's. Exact date unknown.

27.,28.,29.,&30.Reba Richardson,xxx Fae Richards, and Fred DeShields at a party Miss Ric hards threw f or her sister in1935. These pictures are thought to have been taken by Martha Page,

31.Martha and Fae at home.(mid-1930's)

32.Mattha Page. Publicity photo. Silverstar Studio. 1935.

33.Fae Richards. 1936. Publicity photo widely circulated at the time.

34.&35.Fae Richards, Martha Page and unidentified actress on the set of "Raising Cara". 1936. A Silverstar Production. Richards played the uppity servant gxxgirl 'Sara'.

36.Filmstill. "Mr.Owens Meets His Match". 1937. The picture starred Leslie Randall and Thornton Van Clyde. Fae Richards was featured as 'Alice', the faithful Southern servant girl. 'Alice' tries to protect her employer fr om the wiles xxof a young and beautiful golddigger.

37.&38.Filmstills from "<u>Plantation Memories</u>". Silverstar. 1937. Starring Ward Harrison, Bebe Muller, and Fae Richards as 'Elsie - the Watermelon Woman'. This film was an enormous success and Fae received much favorable notice in the press. She became known popularly as the 'the Watermelon Woman', and in fact much of the press from that time refers to her simply as 'the Watermelon Woman', dispensing with her real name altogether.

39.&40.Fae Richards(center), as she appeared in a screentest for the film "<u>Merry-Go-Round</u>", which was never completed. Under pressure from both Fae Richards and Martha Page to give Richards a 'leading lady' role, the character of a young vaudeville dancer was written into the screenplay. Willa Clarke (on Fae's right) was cast as Fae's dance partner and sidekick. The script went through numerous revisions and the title was changed to "<u>That Voodoo Magic</u>". Fae's part was cut back to little more than a cameo, with her dancing in several different 'jungle' costumes while Cassandra Brooke sang the title song, originally written for Fae. Fae left Silverstar Studio during filming, breaking her contract and severing all ties with Hollywood, including her relationship with Martha Page.(1938)

41.,42.,&43.Fae Richards as photographed by Max Hetzl (Monsieur Max). 1938. Max was the in-house photographer for Silverstar Studio and also a good friend of Fae's. Fae posed for these photographs privately, in an attempt to show H.R.Ransin, the studio head, that she could play a leading lady. The studio never allowed these photographs to be released, claiming they "clashed" with the "Watermelon Woman" image. Ransin offered Miss Richards more money and a new contract to appear as a mammy in another Southern melodrama, but she refused.

44.Fae Richards signs contract with J.Liberty Wells, President of Liberty Pictures, a 'black-cast' film studio in Philadelphia, (photo from a Philadelphia newspaper.1940.)

45.Fae Richards, with members of the Philadelphia chapter of the NAACP.(March 1940)

46.Fae Richards and Liberty Wells on location. June 1940.

47.,48.,49.,50.,&51.Fae Richards, circa 1940. Photographs are unsigned, but are attributed to Kenny Long.

52.&53.Scenes from "<u>Souls of Deceit</u>". 1941. Starring Fae Richards and J.Liberty Wells, who also directed the picture.

54.Publicity photo circa 1941. Kenny Long, photographer. Long was a popular black photographer who did most of the studio photography and filmstills for Liberty Pictures.

55.Fae Richards at an art opening for the internationally acclaimed Black sculpterss ,Zola Hamilton. (pictured with Hamilton.) 1941.

56.Unidentified friend.(No date-late'40's or early '50's)

57.Filmstill. "Mr. and Mrs. Big." Liberty Pictures. 1942. Comedy.

58.&59.Scenes from "Black Guns". 1944. Fae Richards and Ray Blake. Fae starred as the sultry gangster's moll, Mattie Cooper. It is her most complex and well-known role in race films and elevated her to household-name status among black audiences. Unfortunately, it was also her last film. Liberty Pictures went bankrupt in 1945.

60.,61.,62.,&63. Fae Richards. Performing "when Things Go Blue" at The Standard.1946. After Liberty Pictuers fold ed, Fae returned to the stage, performing regularly on Philly's South Street, as well as the Horseshoe Club in Harlem, and other venues in Cleveland, Baltimore, and St.Louis.

64.Fae Richards (center) with unidentified friends. circa 1946.

65.,66.,&67. Fae Richards an d June Walker.1955. Fae's 47th birthday party at their home in their home in West Oak Lane, Philadelphia. According to Fred DeShields, Fae and June met while Fae was singing at the Standard. June sat at a stageside table every night for months, always with a white rose for Fae. By 1947, they were living together, and they lived together until Fae's death in 1974, at age 66.

68.June Walker. 1962. Fae's x nickname for June was "Champ".

69.&70. Fae Richards and June Walker. No date. (late '60's)

71.&72.Fae Ric hards. 1971.

73.Fae Richards. 1973. Photo signed Leslie Thomas. The last known photograph of Fae.

FAE RICHARDS IS A FICTIONAL CHARACTER CONCEIVED BY CHERYL DUNYE. ZOE LEONARD PHOTOGRAPHED AND CONSTRUCTED THIS ARCHIVE TO TELL RICHARDS' STORY. THE CAST AND CREW LISTED BELOW STAGED EVENTS FROM RICHARDS' LIFE FOR LEONARD'S CAMERA. THE PHOTOGRAPHS WERE THEN USED AS SOURCE MATERIAL FOR A "DOCUMENTARY" OF FAE RICHARDS' LIFE IN DUNYE'S FILM "THE WATERMELON WOMAN" (1996).

CAST IN ORDER OF APPEARANCE

REBA RICHARDS	L. M. DORIA ROBERTS
FRED DESHIELDS	ROBERT REID-PHARR
FAE RICHARDS	LISA MARIE BRONSON
OSCAR WILLIAMS	KEYLAN BRADLEY
EDWARD VANCLYDE/GRIP/THORNTON VANCLYDE	MARK BREITENBERG
ELEANOR VANCLYDE	NORA BREEN
IRENE VANCLYDE/CASSANDRA BROOKE	SARA VOGT
PARKER VANCLYDE/MAN AT HOLLYWOOD GALA	CLAUDINE BENOIT
ELEANOR VANCLYDE'S GUEST	LINDA SALERNO
MARTHA PAGE	ALEXANDRA JUHASZ
HAIR STYLIST	LUCIANA MOREIRA
SANDRA VINCENT	KRISTINA DEUTSCH
GRIP/STARLET AT HOLLYWOOD GALA	LILY MARNELL
BOBBI/DYKE#1 AT HOTSPOT	VALERIE MANENTI
BLACK GAY MAN AT PARTY	JODY BENJAMIN
JOSIE/WILLA CLARKE	FAWN MCGEE
HAMBONE JONES	REGGAE GRIFFIN
DYKE#2 AT HOTSPOT	ZOE BISSELL
DYKE#3 AT HOTSPOT	JULIA ZAY
WHITE ACTRESS IN "RAISING CARA"	CAROLYN SHAPIRO
J.LIBERTY WELLS	K. BRENT HILL
NAACP MEMBER/RAY BLAKE	KENRICK CATO
NAACP MEMBER #2	DARRELL MOORE
ZOLA HAMILTON	EDITH DUNYE
WOMAN AT OPENING/IN AUDIENCE	EVE OISHI
UNIDENTIFIED FRIEND	JACQUI BISHOP
BLACK DYKE ON ROOF #1	CATHY MCKINLEY
BLACK DYKE ON ROOF #2	CHERYL DUNYE
JUNE WALKER	CHERYL CLARKE

CREW

PRODUCER	CHERYL DUNYE
DIRECTOR	ZOE LEONARD
EXECUTIVE PRODUCER	ALEXANDRA JUHASZ
PHOTOGRAPHER	ZOE LEONARD
PHOTOGRAPHER'S ASSISTANT	KIMBERLY PEIRCE
LIGHTS	CLAUDINE BENOIT
	CHRIS DANIELS
WARDROBE	ALISON FROLING
	SARA VOGT
MAKE-UP/HAIR	LUCIANA MOREIRA
	LILY MARNELL
PROPS	JULIA ZAY
	ZOE BISSELL
SETS	ZOE BISSELL
	LILY MARNELL
	JULIA ZAY
PRODUCTION COORDINATOR	PETRA JANOPAUL
	SHU HUNG
PRODUCTION ASSISTANT	CHARLENE GILBERT
DARKROOM	ZOE LEONARD
	VIVIAN SELBO
	JACK LOUTH
	LISS PLATT
	ANN RUARK
	ELAINE PORTIER
	AMY STEINER
	DIANA MORROW
	ELIZABETH GRIGGS
PRODUCTION STILLS	AMY STEINER
	VALERIE CASEY
	ERICA FREUDENSTEIN
CRAFT SERVICES	MARK BREITENBERG
	EVE OISHI

ARTSPACE BOOKS IS A FORUM FOR CONTEMPORARY ARTISTS AND WRITERS. THESE COLLABORATIONS OF IMAGE AND TEXT BY TODAY'S MOST INNOVATIVE ARTISTS CHALLENGE THE CULTURE IN WHICH WE LIVE, AND INSCRIBE THE VITAL SOCIAL FUNCTION OF ART.

PREVIOUSLY RELEASED FROM ARTSPACE BOOKS:

MEMORIES THAT SMELL LIKE GASOLINE
BY DAVID WOJNAROWICZ

JERK
ART BY NAYLAND BLAKE
FICTION BY DENNIS COOPER

REAL GONE
ART BY JACK PIERSON
FICTION BY JIM LEWIS

DESIRE BY NUMBERS
ART BY NAN GOLDIN
FICTION BY KLAUS KERTESS

THE STRANGE CASE OF T.L.
ART BY TONY LABAT
TEXT BY CARLO McCORMICK

APPENDIX A:
BY A.M. HOMES

FRIENDLY CANNIBALS
ART BY ENRIQUE CHAGOYA
TEXT BY GUILLERMO GÓMEZ-PEÑA